CW00547927

Poetry Romances

THE HEART

Author

MICHAEL GREEN

Charleston, SC
www.PalmettoPublishing.com

Poetry Romances The Heart

Copyright © 2022 by Michael Green

All rights reserved.

No portion of this book may be reproduced, stored in a retrieval system, or transmitted in any form by any means–electronic, mechanical, photocopy, recording, or other–except for brief quotations in printed reviews, without prior permission of the author.

First Edition

Hardcover ISBN: 979-8-88590-810-8
Paperback ISBN: 979-8-88590-811-5
eBook ISBN: 979-8-88590-812-2

Table of Contents

Thanks to, https://images.unsplash.com/photo-1575343661961-396d02abf317?ixid=MnwxMjA3fDB8M
HxwaG90by1wYWdlfHx8fGVufDB8fHx8&ixlib=rb-1.2.1&auto=format&fit=crop&w=750&q=80

PROPOSAL

in your eye's innocence, loves precious peace dances
your pretty smile, lights the sky
with this beautiful pearl, every precious breath soothes
it's so sweet, my spirit and hearts moved
which causes waterfalls of graceful hugs
in such romance, your fragile kisses massage my cheeks
endless beauty you are, and upon it tickles
therefore, this love we have is always in my
heart, emotions, body and mind
therefore, besides there won't be any other in my eye
which is reason I have the in & out most pretty princess
oh my dear, blessings are your fragile and tender kisses
to always have is why you can be confident, in leaning on me
just the taste of this rich and sweetly sexy moisture, has me down on one knee
meaning my adorably precious love, will you marry me

dreams of pretty smile, tickle and enhance emotions
your beautiful heart colors, as if it's a rainbow of oceans
here and now is when all throughout body and mind thoughts of, flourish happiness
therefore, blossoms such pleasing finesse
yes, yes baby, this delicacy en1chants one's inner being
and it is, your incredible all-around beauty has me always singing
therefore, it be true in, out and all around your peace glimmering character, up and down
flourishes our upcoming tree
overflowing friendship our love has, because, from your lips to mine runs the river of beauty
such a bond will always keep us together
beautiful art, reason our love solid lock is why besides you I don't want another

my beautified candy, sexy is the shape of your body
while being felt emotions race with flavors that excite me
with a passionate river of delicious liquid, nothing can be but still
frozen from the taste brings comfort and chills
no kidding but amazing is the astonishment heart, mind, butt and shape cause
have no fear, there's not one thing I can ever find, which will make me pause
at what, my hunger for relationship

Michael Green

that's the beyond beautiful riches that feeds our friendship
because it's you one never wants to lose
when the time of eyes locking has caused no one else, to be who I choose
pretty princess one ponders of some time ago the options, were many but baby I looked within
and am awakened from your beauty
yes sweetie the positivity within heart is what ones character feeds
the caused ongoing joy, is what's strived for you to see
it's all because of the beyond beautiful princesses spirit feed glee
my love, better than does not and never will exist
which is why, our hold must not be missed
therefore. from that first to life's end, just you are it
and such is because my candy you're start and finish
which means reason you're my pretty princess I've come in first place, which shall last for all days
such a know is best because it's not a phase
for forever I'm your property which has been given to
just you
reason you alone are my one and only beauty
which is why I yearn we blossom fruit from our tree
not any other has the gears, like you sweet and sexy

tender kisses you give, and to always enjoy is why I live
beauty blessed beats you shine, and is why one hungers no ending time
caused happiness develops in, which is surely the always desired win
dear sexy love others been seen but enjoyed was the best and reason for I'm in a comfortable rest
so sexy peach there need not be any thought of me wanting another, because I have the best at
my opened door
and reason I'm entirely satisfied, to just feel your body satisfies me higher than the sky
now sweetly fragile gift, for what's been no others come close to the lift
having and holding you caused such a mysterious romance, and it's for that my heart and
emotions shall always dance
here we sit and have determined our steps ahead, by choosing our relationship is the head
the joy we are has blossomed beyond beautiful flowers, and it is why our friendship will never
go sour
explanation of your love just cannot be, the mystical surges or jolts one to an area which
dumbfounds me
a great comfort of love our partnership brings, ands
reason my heart always sings
which is because of fact you are my partner, by which has caused grounds of not desiring any other

it's on day bay basis our teamwork's enjoyed, and reason we always grow is because of wasteful
distractions are avoided
is it yet understood just or only you myself hungers, there be no existence of embracing another
and there just can't be another kiss which comes close
to your caused pleasure, sexy baby with our teamwork
carries us to grow farther
meaning sexy babe because I've been awarded with the
best being you, there's no more for me to choose

face shines pretty flowers, which one's never seen before
princess's gorgeousness always rockets me north
it's the light, which is one of a kind
fragile art, the sexy and special body is so, so fine
as time passes by deep in core, such unique beauty uproots
the special and delicate gift you are
because your lungs disperse rainbow of colors, peace is enjoyed
the vibrant glow, comes from each heartbeat
your graciousness blesses, such friendly emotions
reason that pretty gift my hunger feeds
day by day the obsession to feel, gives ground to my mission
sich is because, your glorious land has no possible finish
and it's why I do not desire any other
also reason why I will not wed another

HANDS WERE DESTINED TO LOCK

It's in, flowers always blossom
Which is why, when called one always come
My heart, princess's flowers pollinate
Such is high grade yes babe nothing but an A
Ands reason your heartbeats, in one's file
When hungry, there's surety you're dialed
Meaning my obsession of you, in my heart, and mind will always be
For me, it's a blessing to taste, touch, feel and kiss the gifts body
So, so specials body, it's true you my gift, flavored peace does please
Yes, sexy babe, for life, in, out, and all around you my delicacy, I need
Therefore, for us to hold one another, for all life's lasting is what excites me
And you must know on me, you can ALWAYS lean
It's simple in and out, you shine the innocence, of a tender dove
Which is why, one's hunger's for princess to feel, enjoy, embrace, and hold, my ALWAYS
lasting love

such the perfect gift you are, it's easy to see you from afar
the blessing always brought causes fulfillment, ands reason for you I would travel that lifelong mile
such passionate love's our locking bond, and shall keep us together, forever ever long
and with one another, the embracing times will always be, so fulfilling equals no mystery

I do see, in you is the home for me
It's true, open are my doors, which await you, my key
Yes sweet blessing, reason your beauty, my spirit sings
Such giddy joy's so awakening, which is why it's you sweet blessing I don't want self-missing
Open your arms whenever hungry, and just know I, you shall see
Which is why, with me, you never feel as if you're alone
Reason the presence of my romancing love, shall always have you feel at home
Here we are, and in me, fire for you has its ground
Therefore, it's the must that you, my precious pearl, hear my soothing sound
It runs throughout you and I, why is why beautiful jewels of love, be our scout
It's my drive and know, blessings shall always be, as we achieve each of life's steps
And I know our love's going to be, so intense I'm proudly going to claim, 'you I kept'

Tick tock, tick tock time passes by, and I desire for us to build and grow
It's my know, our connection shall put on the show
You see my sexy blessing it's true, for all of life's length on me you can rest your heart
Meaning when game, I'm ready to start

In our life's there's going to be journeys
Meaning, on one another we must rely and lean
Within us there's fun awaiting
Ready to fire, and have its lifting
Growth of our bond, and in this treasures shall shine
When such arrives, I just know you and I shall have, endless fun
Our hold of one another, for sure to have lifelong last
Why I just know, you're better than the best

Smile, yes blessing cheek to cheek do so
Therefore, beauty is, and this I know
Reason be, your light excites
This glee filling happy peace, is such soothing light
You girl be so beautiful, so sweet, so delicate and fragile
Heart to heart, spirit to spirit, precious you're always on speed dial
Smile, yes blessing my heart hungers to dance.
You can trust me, meaning after once, I not need another chance
Our tie's happy, reason our sight and plans, has me see children
Which is why after experiencing many journeys, reason our warmth, I'm confident
These confirming grounds provide know, relaxing in my hold shall leave no dents
And in return, our friendship betters the mission, of you and me
Two as one, defines our key
Such passion paves the path, for our upcoming steps
This course has life-long guarantee, which has me feel better than the rest
It's in our formed path we enjoy and taste of that, which others know not of
Such truth has reason, and why you and I kiss and hug

our teamwork is meant to be
for you dear, I would dive to the bottom of sea
in my eyes, for your heart, blossoms gorgeous flowers
It's obvious for you, my feelings aren't sour
it is, my dear princess, within each smile, graces innocence flows
and towards your precious light, I must go

sweetie from you to I, I to you, such fire burns
therefore, my special piece of love, for your body I yearn
and baby, on your lips & cheeks, my lips are
ands reason, your bright shining light's, my happiness and guiding star
oh baby for your touch alone, I'm down on my knees
that's why, always when hungry, you can always rely on me
my pretty pearl it's for you alone, I hunger and thirst
in my heart and mind, you always come first
not one is before, my special gift
which is because, just thoughts of you, give me the fulfilling lift
I hunger to blossom within, life's furthering seeds
there're no words, which have capability to define this upbringing
truth it be, this ongoing jolt, has me always, always singing
it's not possible to define or explain, my horny need for you
ands reason I know, you're the woman I choose
because of you, I've given a finger to all other options
meaning there's been possibilities, but it's my fire for you which had me skip, what got mentioned
as life has its day by day passing, letting you go, I'm not, reason be with you I have joy
which is reason I named you my sexual toy

and baby, it's you who causes overflowing glee, and has me, do the happy dance
do you understand, you babe because your love filling spunk, life provides a last

your jolts bring such waters of love; therefore, I try to have you feel no other card
And why of your mind, body, fire, and heart I will never be tired
yes dear, you are beyond special blessing, and above you there's no one
That's reason, when you in need, towards I come
and in my heart, I proudly claim, it's you, I have
Our tender relationship, will for life last

for you're in my heart, which is food to my passion
therefore day by day, just to kiss is my mission
it need be known it's you, I'm appreciative are mine
for our hold's sassy and naughty, but precise and sweetly fine
which does, and will always maintain eternal last
meaning us always, within one another has solid ground; to be better than the best
such the firm and unbreakable lock's, beat within it's our guarantee
and dear peach, reason that our hold produces majestic glee, which provides life to our giving tree

Dear sweetie, reason be you I have pleasure
Which are thoughts of us being together
Such glee, for me is fulfilling
And with you, because our hold, for all life our hearts will be singing

Your walk has such the delicate melody
Such gracious rhythm has one purpose, to always fertilize our bettering tree
As time passes, I hunger more and more, for your skin
And it's my desire for you to state, 'I desire him'
Which feeds my drive and crave for us to be one; instead of we
Which is my only goal; for sure indeed

Thanks to, https://unsplash.com/photos/500nPYaXoiO

HAPPINESS FLOWS & JOY ENGULFS

Forever girl, I'm your property
Of your fine body, I'm so hungry
It's you I crave
And you baby, I need day by day
Just fall in my arms, & my hold shall be never ending
kissing

Your body, I got hold of
Of you sweetie, I can't get enough
Day by day, I crave your body
Which is reason more and more, to be with you I'm needy
It pleases and betters me, to see, then touch
Which is why, to lick and peer into your body I must
Why such emotions had birth, and must be reason your unique character
Such truths because of your genuinely gorgeous core
And such beautiful light, stems from your heart
And, has you at #1 on my chart

Here times are, with such questions
But just know you are it, because other than you there's not room for another
Why that is, has simple mean, you my beautiful pearl are meant for me
as your so smooth skin meets my lips, my taste's sexual bliss
knowing you and I are together, has me not want any other
there, there are your waves of love, which flood me with more than enough
when it comes to you, taste and tell I do not, don't want to lose what I got
there's never enough of you, for me to enjoy, just use and abuse me as your sex toy
there's no lease, dive in because you get all of me

As I live, thoughts of you has me smile
It's you dear, with my body I desire to tile
And it is, your laughter I hunger for
All by itself, just kn1owing you has me score, score
When I saw you, my heart blossomed joy filling glee
Such uplifting's why I know, you sweetie must be with me
Your body's perfect design, shines candy like comfort
And it's you, I want as my escort

Your life changing & color filling character so, so moves myself
Your uplifting & pretty spirit, shines in self
I've done my looking, & now reason you, my journeys at its end
And why you can rest & know, self can have trust in me, upon you my dear, my words shall
never bend
My endless blessing, embrace my feelings
Sexy peach, as you breathe, to me your cheer always sings
Why I deserve you, really has me, but priceless beauty, I just know you're my gift
It's true, know of you alone has me, always have a lift
And source is, your so, so graceful beauty
And baby girl, it's that alone, which completes me
The tie we have's our endless relationship
In return, to one another's constant blossoming, of our commitment

our light shines bright like the midnight stars
as we grow, more and more our love & lock shows
in this is our beyond beautiful light, which brightens us and guides our sight
such glorious presence of hold is us, and sweet, sweet baby that's our plus
as you breathe, roses blossom
just seeing your pretty face, causes so much fun
such positive light you shine
and that's why you're mine
plans I have for us
we are two, but my dear princess my mission is to make that two one
therefore colors of joy, shall dance in our hearts
so my sexy jewel I'm game and so desire, for you to jump aboard
which is why it's my promise, you sexy gem, rest your heart in my hands, and I shall romance
your spirit
that means with me your joyful and giddy times, have the endless limit
Within your hunger for more, in your eyes passion burns
From our conversing, this I learnt
Romance you strive for, and I'm at your call
Such desire for passion has its furthering joy; which I withhold
In my life just knowing you, day by day's why I smile
And if need be, for you I would endlessly travel mile after mile
These facts of friendships toy, quit often come into play
In comforting form this has me, be driven to please you; for all days

— 9 —

Which doesn't always come as physical relationship, but my whispers massage your spirit
These rewarding tokens, have intention to bring us to enjoying no limit

My only desires to subtract all your depression
Which if game to play, shall have us enjoy, the lifelong connection
Such grip's assuring, to our ongoing relationship
It's our last, which is romances key
And it's why our surety, has me sing in your heart
Your light and delicate words, are the guarantee to harnesses melody
Such majestic rhythm holds your head, and kisses your cheek
Day by day, it's you babe, I hunger to see
And not just the peak
But open the window wide, and allow to shine, your eye bulging beauty
Due to your tie within, on me you can always feed
And for your worthy self, I'm down on my knees
Baby girl, your astounding beauty has me know, you're the gift for me
Because, I deserve only the best
When it comes to you, I pass by the rest

Special cuddle, is our meant mold
In my mind and heart, to you I'm sold
You cause such tender & promising presence
So fantastic you are, and so strong our light, it's not possible for anyone to claim, we're not
meant
In such romance my desire's to, massage and rub
At whatever level between us, it's possible for there to be love

as your so smooth skin meets my lips, my taste is sweet and sassy bliss
knowing you and I are together, has me not want any other
there, there are your waves of love, which flood me with more than enough
it's always more of you I hunger to enjoy, just use me, as your boy toy
there's no lease, dive in, because you get all of me
with me there not be sampling, which means for you, rest in my arms, and on my love you can
always feed

Happiness is comfort, of your soothing touch,
And my dear princess, your beautiful feel I always crave more than enough,
I'm ready to drink, therefore use your juice and fill my cup,

It's clear, you my dear, are the gift of love,
It's my goal to unravel within your heart, and bless with romance,

Which means your cozy comfort, has you in my arms, and brings us to enjoy the eternal dance,
My blessing in you, there's more than enough for me,
For your touch and taste, I'm always needy,
Pretty, such romantic fragrance is your feel,
And knowing another liked you, means I got the steal,

Here we are holding hands
As time ticks by, passing byes life's sand
But with our connection, such passion erupts
It's guarantees, I will never pass up
And then it erupts. that tick tock melody has made its ground
Such peaceful harmony's, our sound, and has rock solid ground

Yo, yo check it, you want best ever, just look in the mirror
The reflection you see's why if not right by, I'm always near
There's no possible explanation, for the gifts you give
Which is reason, in knowing you, is fuel to live

Your shape, has such pleasing finesse, so great, it pushes aside all the rest
Toe to head you're pleasantly perfect, and my sexy blessing I just can't wait, till locking's our connect
As I live, it's you I embrace, such relief has me soar to a giddy length
All in all it's your happiness I see, and those gifts will always keep me
Yes my dear sweetheart, reason your character, to you I'm sold

Be sure to hold my hand, and therefore majestic candy, blossoms within our mold
It's now, and always my sweet peach, you have my full attention
Meaning for you, I have never ending passion
It's each thought of you, that romances me to sleep
In the waking morning, knowing I have friendship with you, brings such keep
To life's mystery, of knowing not my tomorrows
For that joy, has I push forward
Just knowing with you, gift's always awaiting
In me as the ring, ring rhythm, my heart's singing
For you baby's, always a gentle kiss

It's that alone, meaning I can't live, if I miss
To bring me warmth and comfort, your hugs ease my heart
It's that baby girl, which motivates me, day by day to start
And in such cuddling, myself rests
It's our bonding lock, that furthers life in our nest
Such hold's reason it's you I desire in my hold
This awakening joy and glee, peeps haven't been told
I promise peach, stick with me, and you not regret my touch
These happy jolts, happen to excite me
In and out of you is I, so tasty, it be guarantee you always crave my tree
With your smiles, your cheeks light my heart
Rely on and trust in me; therefore with, we begin our fulfilling start
In meaning my feelings for you, are richest pearl's passion; for our forwarding
My promise to you blessing, I shall have you never feel as I, you are missing
It's my guarantee, reason my touch always satisfies
In such the way, as the team, our bond shall always see eye to eye
Sexy girl our loving torch, in no disguise
Therefore, my hold and your feel, brings our bond to have you know, with me you never have to
search or try
My dearest desire is for you to enjoy pleasure
Which is my hearts determination, for sure

It's why you, yes my darling are my happiness and joy overflowing artwork
Overflowing gratefulness floods, as we live out the growth in our teamwork
Meaning the best possible gift, it's you alone I live for, and will always have the urge and hunger
to feed more
Which is why I know met has been the best possible score
Something as simple as your every breath I treasure
Best yet, all distractions our teamwork well past the perfect sheet, does conquer

OUR SEXUAL PLEASURE

So confident it's you, who be my mission,
Therefore, just to feel and kiss is my finish,
And it's you, I whole heartedly hunger,
That sweet, sweet baby, source I know you're my sexy treasure
One which has my full attention, and shall always have all of me
My sweet lullaby it's you and you alone I desire, I strive to please, and of, never grow tired
Have you for full shift, not wanting to let you go, of my endless lift
Your sand of tickles shall, and does romance, and it's hand by hand we're always going to dance

Now baby is it yet clear, I've done my looking, and what I've seen does not measure to your
cooking
It's in you I see such furthering joy, and that my precious, is why of you I shall never tire
You see princess, my romance has such cuddle
You're that sweet blessing who has ground to claim, it's he who's my assuring settle
Our lock always has my hold, for its emotions provide ground to claim, to him I'm sold

Here we are, and it's you, who has my attention
By which means, between us there shall be no tension
Instead, passionate rivers of love, which has me dial into your heart's beautiful eyes
So special and delicate you are, our tender loves in no disguise
Therefore, our harmony shall have life-long hold
And it's my determination, to bring our special times, to shine like gold
We must connect, and have mixture, and in such blessings there's no finish
Which guarantees, to bring you and I better than best win

For it's our connection, which has heart to mind, mind to heart success
You are it, within one another, meaning our conjoining's the perfect fit
For your body alone, erupting are my constant hormones
And such harmony's, for sure never going to leave you, feel alone
Sit in my lap, and let me rub out, all life's cramps
For my caressing alone, will have you feel, that's more than enough
Feel, and hear my words, therefore towards me, you will move closer
If you award me, my touch leaves you, never needing another chance
I'm one shot man, meaning from the beginning, all my love's in
Meaning I take no chances with that one, and it's you

— 13 —

Reason I don't accept anything, but the win
Meaning from the green light, my entire effort's in

It's my romance and emotions, which has you always wanting more
By which means my guidance's for sure to have you feel, that you're reaching the best score
And my tickles, you're always going to want
Which shall have you feel, like not having any other font
It's romances fire, I desire us to share
For with me, you can always rest, in my soothing care
No greater than the other, but on the same page we are
Sweetie that's because in my eyes, you're my only star

As you smile, fulfilling flowers blossom
Which has me, in your direction come, come
Meaning its time, you let them shine
And to see and touch you, is each moments mission of mine
Therefore as the team, or two as one our connection shall begin
And to have you as mine, to I's the win
Such victory, has bright shining beauty
Which has me know, as former seeds, apples shall fall from our tree
In meaning hand to hand and lips on lips, with trust of one another we shall form the bond
And such lock, other than you, there isn't any other thought
In yours and I's assuring hold, is our ongoing passion, which provides endless greens
This producing feed's what shall have you know, it's on I you can always lean

obvious it is, your lips I hunger to kiss
your body excites me, which's why you girl, must be with me
it's true, as you speak love within furthers, and has me know we must be together
my peach it's your character, which excites me, and has result of one seed
these plantations pour from our spirits, which guarantees our relationship have no limit

What we are, has us on an unbreakable love chart
When I saw your beautiful self, the perfect design you have, just teases myself
There's such fire in your **eyes**, which hungers I, to be on your side
It's that truth which always burns, and forever keeps us, in each other's arms
That happy hold's what ties us together, and what forms our connection, closer to loves charm
Such building blocks of life's adventures, form our passage way
And it's this taste which brings I fulfillment, day after day

This satisfaction of your beautiful self, has I enjoy your colors of love
That joyful ride colors like that, of the beauty shining dove
Yes dear I can see in your eyes, such gentle, and loving innocence
Beauty, to be with you, just makes sense
Not mattering time or light, your presence causes such cheer, to flood my heart
And it always fires rockets, and causes, ongoing drive to start
Reason each day is new, and our unity has me, more and more thirst, and hunger you
Therefore it's easy choice for me, you I choose

On going's an inferno fire, and passionate love for you
My precious gift, I like no other, it's you I desire to daily use
And there's surety, it's you I choose
Such promising joy you are, and reason your body's my food, I'm never far

Your happiness is your soothing touch,
And my dear princess your beautiful feel is more than enough,
I'm ready to drink, therefore I use your juice and fill my cup,
It's visibly clear, you are my gift of love,
It's my goal to unravel self, within your heart and spirit,
Which means with cozy comfort, has you in my arms, and brings us to enjoy no limit,
With you blessing, there's more yes more than enough for me,
For your touch and taste, I'm always hungry,
Pretty, such romantic fragrance is your feel,
Your joy's my joy, and my meal,

Hear we are holding hands
As our time ticks by, love furthers life's sand
But with our connection, such hormones erupt
It's a guarantee, of each, you and I shall never pass up
Then tick tock time, has made its ground
Within innocence, peaceful harmony's our sound
Light kisses, your face has, and it honors me that I have privilege to hold you, in my hand
Desiring perfect's reason it's you, which is my goal
This eye awakening joy and glee, thankful I got
I promise stick with my love, and passion for me will birth from want, to must
Your giddy jolts, always excite me
In and out of you is I, therefore it's guaranteed, you're my honey bee

With time passing, more and more feelings for you take shape
Reason be these emotions have such comfort, I know you're no mistake
Ongoing fire's used to blossom one on one seeds, and source being you, majestic fruits shall lifelong be
Your face's greatly rewarding, and has my hearts symphony singing
Such filling joy your words cause, surpasses any other possibility
My dear gift, it's to my heart, you hold the key
Therefore it's you, and you alone, who has me
I look forward to that day, life blossoms from our tree
In such the way harmonizing colors, are that which comfort
The love our lips have, are for only one another, and this truth brings my heart ease
This rock-solid hold's one to keep our lock, so secure there's no desire for another shot

Ongoing salute, from me you have
Can you trust him, some ask
Do you trust yourself
If so, you trust me
Which is cas our steel strong lock, holds us together
Meaning, there not be one situation that has ground to knock over our tower
In such unity, covering you to I and I to you our kisses shower
Such unbreakable warmth, shall keep us hand to hand forever

YOUR SUN LIGHTS & HEART GREATLY BEAUTIFIES

It's always girl, you blessing have me proudly claim, I love her
Meaning my dear sweetie, do you yet comprehend I want you for only me
This means I strongly desire, of me, you're never tired
For life's last luscious love, it's my determination we aren't some
But as the unbreakable team, we are one
In such the hold, our genuine truth shall produce flowers
Therefore that bright shining truth, our teamwork feeds, always displays production of flavor
filled colors

It's simple
Precious cuteness shines, from your sweet dimples
Of course I accept
To me, always you must be kept
As we grow closer and closer, woven treasures between us do, and shall always continue to
blossom
Just know, always with open arms I whisper, come my gift come
You know it, you beautiful blessing you're always a plus
And yes lollipop to lick and kiss you clean, I have in mind to do
That's my key, and has you, with me left to choose
It's true there's no possible outcome of pain with me
With such surety, just know it's you I shall always see
Yes my Lovable peach, your tasty, and naughty spunk I will ALWAYS taste
Meaning girl within one another, our just right font will last for our ongoing tomorrows
And such excitement I cause; when I touch
As our relationship continues, our blossomed fruit, furthers us
As we breathe, our beats have a connecting tie
This joyful passion beauty, has no disguise
My dear beauty, it's simple because there be such fire
It's your hearts ongoing heat, which has me always feel higher and higher
Every song of joy, causes thoughts of you
Such happiness has I know, from spirit to spirit, we phone

Baby girl you are it, no one else but you
Day by day, you are my only study in school
Blessing is, your mind and spirit I've learnt, reason, you I cannot lose
This satisfying answer, me it does amuse
They're no words, which define my feelings, for you
Your smiles, so tickling, for those tokens bring enchantment to I
Such causes reason, day by day I long to look in your eyes
For you, from my heart and mind, my feelings are in no disguise
Just seeing you, brightens my day
Thoughts of holding you, have me know, you're no mistake

For you my dear, thanks and appreciation I'm ALWAYS going to have; which can't be put in words
Such ground has reason, because of our beauty we're always moving forward
This move we take part in, shall continue for eternity
Meaning as life is, forever I in you, forever you in me
This movement is our forwarding motion
Which is like me rubbing and caressing your body, with fulfilling lotion
This walk locks our links we have tied, which passes on in our continuous push for a secure hold
It's with that key we form, that sets our goal
Such passionate love, keeps us together
Ands reason there's no one better, then one another
You got it girl, I just know you're my life long prize
Due to your bright shining beauty, it's not in any disguise

Baby girl, here we are, and it's obvious to me, you sweet love are my gift
My dear love, you're my fulfilling lift
Reason your waves of joy, you satisfy as I sexually am pleased
Pleasure like no other, hungry for more brings me to down on knees
Meaning you plus I, is our joining addition
Such fulfilling times of your presence, romance me as we live out our mission
Therefore blessing of your presence alone, causes from you to I, such ease
Such blessings shall tickle and tease
And now running throughout you, is my joy rushing, and comforting peace
It's now my SO precious peach, our connections shall further
This means it carries us to solid stance of love, which lasts forever and ever

know you're so, so beautiful present always can rest, in my lap
with me, there isn't any conflict; as if you're in a trap

but instead, I shall caress you with romance
which for sure, will always, last

as time passes more and more, I just cannot wait to enter, because I know that lock's secure
which has not yet had anyone's enter, and those grounds is where I hunger to further
because even though opportunities are in hundreds, untouchable's my land
ands reason I'm determined to hold you, hand by hand
which has my hormones burn like the wildfire, and it's true, of you my heat shall never tire
such warmth, meaning loves temp has me always, for you feel on fire
that is just how it is, and that blessing, which is reason you shall always enjoy endless bliss
this comfort does, ands guarantee to carry and comfort, therefore I don't want to miss

It's true, just when you think that taste's complete, piling on are more and more, blessings of me
This intense passion shall hold our love together strong like a Redwood tree
Therefore together, not as two but one we unite, and our bonding key unleashes everlasting
happiness
And this precisely perfect joy, is the guarantee between each other, we shall not miss
Miss what?, our endless relationship, which holds us together
In the strongest lock possible, is what our bond, feathers
Yes, between us is not rough and rocky, but cuddly wuddly
Which is reason why, our love, isn't hard to see

as the wind brushes your face, your adorable smile brings such beauty
in your heart lives my hunger to feed
these tokens shall bring us closer, and closer together
now that you're seen, **find anyone else I don't bother**
such the blessing of so, so precious and adorable love you are
because of your gentle grace, in your eyes shines beyond beautiful stars
that grace, so delicately flows all throughout your face
in this I clearly observe, on your body, delicately woven lace
this remarkable beauty, shines in your every step
for this treasure, shall always be known I kept
in meaning such miracles, cause the tidal wave of blossoming beauty
it's that reason, only you babe to my heart always have the keys

and you see dear, it's you I swear who has my attention
meeting you, is the final lesson
meaning with aim or intention to perfectly please, I study you day and night

your body, mind, character and spirit I memorize
therefore, happy times always dance in my noggin
reason you're fulfilling sparkles, never leave me bumming
instead causes fire, which has me always hopping
I'm always on your side, in meaning me you never have to be finding
perfect gift, towards your glee, I'm always coming

YOUR BLISS IS ENDLESS

our bond's secure, because between us unbreakable love's swinging
such tie, there is between us
this hold we have's, the number one plus
of you, I can't get enough
I have immense comfort, because our relationship is never tough
before you, no one's above
oh, oh my precious rose it's my fire for you, which desires to explode
it's your touch alone, that unlocks my code

it is us, and for one another we shall always be limitless plus
and all distractions, having no care or allowing no interferences, by me are left in the dust
reason you pearl, it's now I see who's always my true choice
with enchanting eyes your beautiful smiles, prevent side wandering and re-routing; towards all
distracting noise
which has me boldly know I'm wise to claim myself, as your boy

as time passes by, thoughts of you arise, and you cheer, I find
therefore blessings of you are bountiful, which causes my heart to be colorful
this means my precious gift, reason be you I always have fulfillment
it's now time you're happy, cas I'm now on one knee
even in the dark, your beauty shines bright
your sparkling eyes, deliver such light
the smile of beautiful fire's, what you have
peace in you, is for sure never going to leave me sad
your skin's smooth like silk
I desire to drink, your tasty milk
dance in your beauties, what I desire to do
face of fragile innocence, belongs to you
such tender skin of yours, I desire to rub
thoughts of joy in me, which's reason I dwell on your glee delivering hugs

it's you my preciously pretty pearl, I'm for sure not going to miss
but you must comprehend, the blessing just to see you, gives my eyes the kiss
such fragile innocence is within your beyond beautiful face
warmth of ease I withhold, which is reason your fiery light is my guide in life's maze

and such beauty, shines in your smile
for you, I would travel planet distance miles
because of you princess, I have the top score
and loving you, shall never be the chore
yes inch by inch, in present my kisses are sown on each priceless heartbeat; of yours
meaning, you're the sweetest and finest; so adorably tender pearl
I'm confident, your beautiful selves what shall ALWAYS hunger my heart
which is cas it's your graceful character that brings me fulfilling comfort
upon my spirit and heart, so strong is you, it burns
that's because your passionate sweet, sweet romance. loving you is always on mind
which leaves me, not hungry for any other kind

loving light is our hold
which causes us to never give and fold
here we are, and as we grow closer my joy filling passion furthers
such fire of emotions, your twinkle covers
wrap me, of our promising future
therefore, reason be your fragile touch I luster

you cause me, in such harmony to smile
ands why I programmed, when wanting happiness, you I dial
sweetie not hormones but feelings I have for you, are so immense
and from what I see, you to being it, just makes sense

reason be beauty, which your heart is, has no definition
therefore my doors are open, for you to enter, and I want you to fill the open section
which means it's vitally necessary, you feel me, and jump aboard
meaning you as I, I as you must be our final score
it's in that bond, and reason our joy feeds us, of each other, we need more and more
as the sun shines, your smile brightens me
having one on one relationship with you, inspires my drive to lean
with your each breath, your positive cheer showers my spunk
yes dear, I promise you, you and I will always have intimate fun
I see within your eyes, angel's beauty shines
literally there's no possible explanation, that explains my glee filling appreciation, of knowing
you sweet cheeks; are mine
reason upon you, day and night my heart pours love

which has you shine, the innocence of a dove
and in this peace, great cheer shines in your every step
that's another reason, I have gratefulness, it's you I kept
which is just one reason there's praise to you, for your body
such the blessing's you, meaning you dear, conclude me
my feelings have intention to romantically tease you
one on one time, leaves me not wanting any other
these jolts leave me knowing, forever it's you I choose

to touch, hug and kiss your body is best blessing; all on its own
for its obvious fact: you for me, me for you before time has been sown
and yes pretty pearl, I can see it's you I immensely hunger to caress and rub
just seeing you has me know, of you I can never get enough
because it's from your body the richest taste exists
there's confidence in knowing it's you, you sexy gift I don't want to miss

reason be your smiles alone, romance my body, and spirit
such cozy innocence has me know, the everlasting glee you bring, has the reach of no limit
in meaning, such an amazing gift, you are
far past the best's your friendly charm
and reason your sweet, sweet smiles. tears I display
thankful I am your happiness can be, for all days

greatest gift you are
amazing is your friendliness, so pleasing, it can't be put on any chart
then there's your tender body
that delicate gift feeds fruit; as if it's the tree
which provides the richest foods
and reason that, most definitely=you I choose
as I lick your body, enjoyed is massive bless, and feeling your skin's beginning of my meal
so round from breast to breast, my hands rotate like wheels
point being made fulfillment I have with you
that pleasure has me know it's only you I use
in our teamwork, our hands are locking
meaning never again, for the genuine man, do you have to be looking
it's I, who always be there, to lean on
guarantee is, with me you're always going to be my one

sweet precious, you're my only
always having your sexy self on mind, leaves no time for weeds
meaning sexy you, and you alone are my choice
now my dear plus after plus, you're it as my voice
sweetening's our sassy music
for it fulfills and causes such awesome amusement
there's passion we have, and grounds for more pleases
satisfaction of you, is my fire, and has me think of your peaches
and yes it's here and now I'm in awe of your fragile innocence
and it's our locking bond, by which makes perfect sense
understandable to that which colors; meaning brightens our long-lasting lock
it's now my pretty flower, trust, and into my arms fall off the dock
because it's with this tie, you shall see
view into my heart, which is one to have, know you can trust me
my dear blessing, for you I'm down on my knees
just reach out, because for you, my heart's key
and with this hold, our seeds shall blossom
which has me with open arms say, come, come, oh yes you hottie unto me come, come
that's reason, it's you my dear I long to hold more and more
it's in my know, you my love are easily my exquisite score
the best's not rare jewels, but my sexy sweetie it's you
only wanting first in line is me, which is why, you I choose
such the easy decision I have
which leaves me so, so glad
day by day, and night by night my passionate fire brings happiness
my fire's you, and always has me have the best
by which means when you hungry, on me you can feed
and my meals, shall leave you never in need
meaning by such joy, I have fun with you my toy
therefore it's I you shall keep and for all life, to tickle and tease, I shall be your boy

loves harmony colors our hearts
ands reason, we never again, have to start
it's easy to comprehend, fulfilling beauty is our fuel
and is why our feelings, shall defeat any duel
our time together shall excite, and avoid any lies
because our genuine lock, has buried any disguise

yes my blessing, just like children our furthering shall bring us smiles
that guarantees to push aside, all life's trials
and surely our bonding hold, is our genuine mold
our pure and delicate grip, has lasting hold
in your heart, lives gear to my start
baby girl it's fact you're number one, on my chart
just having you, brings me tears
and these waters of glee, shall be for life long years
Which causes, your lips to be sweetening candy, and breath of honey satisfies
yes dear, in you is fulfillment, and my feelings have no disguise

having, holding, kissing, and seeing you so pleases, and satisfies my heart
and why I'm so grateful, you gave me the start
such appreciation I have
there's just nothing better than your heart, and hand
yes baby it's you who always, will have me
it's you're in and out beauty, that's my heart's, golden key

Blessings are sudden, when sight of you is
Such warmth, brings I remarkable bliss
You're each laugh, colors my heart with love
Which brings me to placing no other above
Do you yet understand, for me you are nothing but the best
And you cause self, to feel better than the rest

as your hair brushes in wind, it's clear reason I have you, causes the win
this charges happiness, which causes our bond to never endure loneliness
therefore fulfilling seeds begin to open, which's why we're even
you see sexy, for punishment you're bending over my knee, and feeling me
now that better be my final warning, but if not, you catch one; when not expecting
our time together will produce such delightful fruit, by which means, we shall feed off one
another
our words are guaranteed to be straight up, and we always provide, likable sum

AND LOVES COVERING BLOSSOMS

sweetie I SO, SO hunger for more and more of your body, reason it's the obsession of me
with that I can't get enough, of who you are, for from your heart, shines love beyond beautiful
charm
totally awesome find you are, meaning your glossiness pleases me from near and afar

just knowing I have you, heals each past scar
what you are to me, by myself can't be understood
not able to comprehend, what your touch withholds, it's so comforting it just has me in the state
of unknown
that time in life, permanently within I, myself has sown
and just when I think stillness is, is when the blessing has presence, of your kiss
and so full of beyond beautiful love, understanding I always miss
so my precious love, it's you my dear who has me
that's right, you shall always be my key
and therefore within you, shall develop into whole, my installed seeds

your perfect beauty, withholds no definition
you have me, piece by piece section by section
it's these times when we connect, and I feel your indescribable self, I begin to understand
you might question me on what's up, but I strive because myself is your number one fan
you see it's in your cheeks, and smile where much, much innocence exists
and from within your eyes, endlessly pours out earth shaking bliss
and it's that, I refuse to miss

such movement some don't feel, but how you yourself can withhold this life, still has my
comprehension in pieces
but because I'm so hungry, ongoing is my feed
tasting your down below and up above juice, does please
and that be why, you can always count on me
my so, so special, and pieced together love, that's my promise
dear blessing I shall always leave you, with nothing but better than best
your undefinable and satisfying self, deserves better than what's best to offer
but I promise you, what I have awaiting's much, much better
and myself does grasp, onto taste of your beyond beautiful custard
because girl you must know, we shall succeed the better than, top of line score

which most definitely, within my heart and mind's the fire that needs more and more
and yes your presence alone, causes jewels of beauty, to be shining
and sweet lullaby, just trust and receive, therefore there's no more climbing

Thanks to, https://images.unsplash.com/photo-1556019540-92288e39ec50?ixid=MnwxMjA3fDB8M
HxwaG90by1wYWdlfHx8fGVufDB8fHx8&ixlib=rb-1.2.1&auto=format&fit=crop&w=750&q=80

Our hold of one another must, must not break, because promising is our wake
Our atmosphere provides such warmth, which has us towards one another come forth
As time passes our hugs and kisses have the tie, and this sweetie's in no disguise
As I taste you, myself likes the lollipop, therefore feelings increase
This sense brings my emotions, such ease
Our forever lasting love's where our beauty shines, which always has me at the table; ready to dine
Your body is my meal, and your emotions I savor like the endless wheel
Wheel of water and flavor, you're the surety of never being sour

as the light leaves and night comes, it's not hard to see because your loving character brightens,
to taste, and touch you, be guaranteed to bring me bliss
just thinking of fun you and I can have, brings me such excitement
it's for that reason I know us together, is and has always been meant
for us to have something, we both must swim same seal
therefore there's rain of comfort and sun of love, between us
which causes, rainbows colorful plus
in meaning our relationship holds, and has promising ground
firmness that's a 100% guarantee to please, which is reason our passions erupting sound

here time is and days pass, and sweetie have you seen your fine, back class
because I have and my eyes are awake to what is meaning there be no possibility, you, I ever miss
I mean it's your smile and glimmering eyes, those gifts are higher than the highest sky

You my dear, drive me to another gear
Therefore it's you who takes my breath, you sweetie who has me kept
For life I want no other but you, baby girl you are who I choose

Your perfect character's so precise
For us, as the couple, side by side
Which delivers, the so comforting and pleasing light
Such awakening has the excitement of your curves, which satisfy my sight
Your body's so fine
It has such sweet, sweet and sassy design
As I look in your eyes, you're the one I desire
During day, and at night, my eyes hunger to get lost in you
Dear special baby your each heartbeat, glistens my spirit
And you fine lady, with you our destiny shall reach no limit
Now you sexy fox, hear me clearly I desire for you and myself to have something
Just cling to me, and you shall always be resting
Kiss on your neck, and find that special spot is my crave
I promise you precious blessing, you're not making a mistake
Time passes by, and there must not be anymore
Right now, right here just look in the mirror
Your pretty fire shines so bright: it's far, and near
Unbreakable light's, within every smile
Through those gifts shine rivers of love, which has me for you, passion to, over and over swim
the Nile

Not mattering if I'm far away, to see your light, for the beaming blessings aren't hard
You see girl, just you taking breath by breath has you in first place on my score card
But that's not it, because to be with your tender and delicate self, shall always unleash, the most satisfying finesse
And that my most adorable pretty pearl, I 100% for sure, don't want to miss

Thanks to, https://images.unsplash.com/photo-1526353043579-c836f1c675ad?ixid=MnwxMjA3fDB8M HxwaG90by1wYWdlfHx8fGVufDB8fHx8&ixlib=rb-1.2.1&auto=format&fit=crop&w=334&q=80

Kiss after kiss, our feelings increase
It's that reason alone, which has I withhold desire to please
Lightning of love, and rain of joy
For your perfectly pretty sunlight, is my day by day toy
Which shall bring us, girl after girl, and boy after boy
you my precious pearl, bring my discomfort rest
and sweetie, such luxury it is; meaning you, you pretty pearl are better than the best
with your presence of joy and sparks of fire, you my dear Love, put myself in another gear
which has me smiling and is reason why, I always want you closer than near
meaning I shall have the beyond beautiful blessing of feeling you
that feel, my passionate lullaby leaves me knowing there's no one else but you; to choose
just to kiss you, and rub your skin puts me on high honor
it's a jolly guarantee this high feel, shall leave me never feeling sour
I do not and cannot comprehend how such beauty you are, even exists
for perfect gorgeousness, your name is #1 on the list
for me, with sight of you, jolly glee erupts
this easements warmth, is such the plus
and then it's their waves of cheer which flow in your smiles
truth has ground in the fact, for your kisses I always hit redial
girl it's true, just sight of you puts me in pause
the rocketing fire within your pretty cheer, is cause
when low thoughts of you, ease my mind
the feel of your lips, to me is so kind
appreciation I have, because I can claim you as mine
having what we are in present, has me know it's not possible to be better than this time
it's also why I'm sure, in you dear is easily the best find
and stemming from our light, is reason our unity is, never going to be in the bind
therefore it must be known day by day thoughts of you bring me such peace
It's that delicacy, which is my ongoing treat
and be reason it's your hand I desire to always hold
which is why I know, so beautiful shall be our mold
yes girl, with you baby I desire to have more than one
and with you girl I make sure to make our life together, genuinely fun
in me constant is reason for our love
which is constantly feed of you, has me feel above
it's true just to see or think you, tickles my heart
and is reason, with you in new activities I'm always ready to start
such fuel is why to touch and taste you, I need more, more

always winning's only reason you precious love, are always my score
with that settling, I find everlasting peace in your hold
your hugs alone is why, pretty princess you're always my goal
my dear princess, you and I who make the perfect mold
for your mind, and heart, sweet and sexy I'm sold
that guarantee's my promise to you, you and I for all eternity
that be it, which's cas you're the one and only girl I see

your body alone my peach is reason why I crave your taste
and has me hungry for you; for all days
you as my woman, is no waste
it's so engulfing, I know, for you this fire within is no phase
but's reason I continuously reach for more, more of you
which has my ground in knowing for the most stupendously special: it's you I choose

Thanks to, https://images.unsplash.com/photo-1517607648415-b431854daa86?ixid=MnwxMjA3fDB8M
HxwaG90by1wYWdlfHx8fGVufDB8fHx8&ixlib=rb-1.2.1&auto=format&fit=crop&w=1492&q=80

it just is, like the wind carries from your heart to mine, dances such bliss
which's key reason I'm 100% sure, choice of you I didn't miss
in relation with waters covering, so wonderful yourself is, your blessings cover
this settling warmth's reason why, I surely don't want any other
like leaves color the air, your breath paints art on my heart
That's one and only reason finding you, has you as #1 on my score card

what we have has lifetime lasting
yo, yo baby it's, from me to you I'm surely not passing
reason be, it's with you heart to heart I'm dancing
this is cas, it be you I'm always thinking
your each step pleases me and reason be such tickles I enjoy
is it now understood by you, you baby causes me such joy

our relationships tickled and kissed with such engulfing love
and it's you my dear charm who will never have any other above
meaning to all the distractions with great might I shove
my precious pearl your hearts fulfillment shines the peace of a beyond beautiful dove
it's you babe who has my heart
and such appreciation I have you've given me the start
better than you, I know it is not possible
in fact even in the same scale isn't plausible
my love the possibility of understanding your in and out charm overwhelms my heart with joy
which is why my so special delight I have appreciation I can call you my toy

Thanks to, https://images.unsplash.com/photo-1500900173725-e0978c945e23?ixid=MnwxMjA3fDB8
MHxwaG90by1wYWdlfHx8fGVufDB8fHx8&ixlib=rb-1.2.1&auto=format&fit=crop&w=751&q=80

I JUST DON'T COMPREHEND YOUR SWEETNESS

we are two, but my dear princess my mission is to make that two one
therefore colors of joy, shall dance in our hearts
so my sexy jewel I'm game and so desire, for you to jump aboard
which's why, it's my promise sexy gem, rest your heart in my hands and I shall romance you,
to no end
that means with me your joyful and giddy times, for sure shall have the **endless** limit
meaning sexy my mindset has base of you, which supplies ground you are it; for the woman I
choose
I never want another, no restart, different font or color
just how you are I admire, and for all life I desire to love your fire

Meaning passion of me, is to further our mold
In this conjoining, our fiery hold furthers
Our growing brightens our tomorrows
And is guaranteed to fasten, yours and mine sow
You know it peach, it's with you I hunger to hold hands
And forever girl, reason be our feelings in my arms you shall land
Therefore you must have joy, cas for your touch my excitement dances
Just know baby, it's one meaning not knowing with me it shall not be chance after chance
How I view, is blessing you are for sure; which I shall not waist
Therefore my heart to yours, my honesty shall have sealing with our loving paste
And I am sure, on your heart this locking hold shall leave colors of my trace
Which's reason why, you shall never stress or worry; my love has genuine lace

Within your hunger for more, in your eye's passion burns
From our conversing, that I learnt
Romance you strive for and therefore I'm at your call
Such desire for passion has its furthering joy; which I withhold
In my life, just knowing you day by day causes me to smile
In return you, I dial
That's the number to your heart, and is why for you I have plans of romance, on file
These facts of friendships toy, quit often come into play
In comforting form this has me, have passion to please, for all days

Which doesn't always come as physical relationship, but my whispers massage your spirit
And it's these bliss filling tokens, which have intention to bring us to enjoying no limit
My only desires to subtract all your depression
Which if game to play, shall have us enjoy a much holding connection
Such grip is assuring to our ongoing relationship
It's that for sure last, that's romances key
And its reason be this surety, my desires within your heart sing
Words which are a guarantee to harness melody
Rhythm that holds your head, and kisses your cheek
It's day by day you I hunger to see, and not just the peak
But open the window wide, and allow to shine your eye bulging beauty
It's with that love, on me you can always lean
Reason be, your astounding beauty has me know you are the gift for me

Sweet and p.retty you are
When I see you, it's clear you're my star
So life grasping is your cheer
All that and above's you my dear
In our bond, such passion is our hold
Within one another each heartbeat seals the mold
And then as time ticks by, in each step forwarding tickles develop
Baby girl who is secure love of my life, it be you which with me has duplicating direction
Think, think away cas it's my goal, to make more of us
Having our appearance alone, the locking beauty we are is always the plus
It is that, all by itself which promises our joy to succeed
the success shall be met in such deeds
For sweet passionate love you are, as time has its day by day passing, my fire for you is more and
more hungry
It's this, which causes your taste of honey
You got girl, it's your lips which sooth and comfort
And is my resting port
As time passes by, it's for you, you sweet blessing I yearn
Yes sweet baby, I've made my mind up you're my final score
Sweetie, on my mind you touch and kiss, there's no one else but you
This gear has I know it's because of you I have the win

Such victory has I always feel like the winner; at the finish
It's you, who has brought me such times of joy, and happiness

And in such the gear's our beautiful outpouring kiss
Days did pass and for you I stood
Hearing from you, rebuilt my wood
Which brought firm assurance in my know
And that confidence is what I use to sow

For you, from my spirit and heart my love is flooding
Which shall always have me not want to be choosing
Such immense emotions cover me with your beauty
And that my pretty princess has me just know it's with you I desire to build the tree
In such spoiling you dear have my word, I'm always on your side
Which is cas just your gorgeous glow, brings me the highest high

My hold and your feel bring our bond to have you know, with me you never have to search or try
And my precious, just know it's in my arms you can always lie
Which's cas my dearest desires for you, to enjoy pleasing pleasure
And it's you I whole heartedly want, and it's that sweet, sweet baby; which has me know you're
my sexy treasure
That know is my reason, it's you sweetie who has me in check
Which causes constant blossoming of blessings, and defeats possibility of there being any mess
Here and now is when I can proudly claim, you I love
That's to right, to left, below and above

you sweet pearl, are it
knowing with you in my arms, is the satisfying finish
which brings my fulfillment, that has happiness; of no limit
on your each cheek and lips I desire to kiss
and it's those thoughts alone, which provide ongoing cheer
and has me know it's you dear, who's my one and only gear

After seeing you, moisture's trickling from my lips
And resting in my satisfaction of you, such rhythmic bliss
These waves of love, lock our unity
For it's our ever-flowing partnership, which furthers passion, of our destiny

stars light the sky, and you brighten my heart
I'm ready to start, my dear be open there's no need to hide
☺☺=☺

just listen to the waters of my heart to mind, that lock's my guarantee
and precious it's simple to use my key, it withholds your character traits; which are so, so kind
☺☺=☺

just rest and hear, for my sound's easily comprehend-able
to rub and massage you I'm capable, fire to please you is limitless year
☺☺=☺

in you is my passion, and you know both sections
so nice is our time cas it has no tension, your happy light gives me the lesson
☺☺=☺

as we hold one another, we intertwine, and this passion tickles me like the feather
as your heart beats I can claim it's love I heard, such bond has me not want any other
☺☺=☺

there from your mouth pours that tasty score, and it's you I am drawn towards
as you lay in my arms our bond brings us forward, your delicious body is always the A++ tour
☺☺=☺

your character's easy best plus, it's not tough cas gorgeous rose the gift is you
it's true as the present you came, which didn't leave me the same
☺☺=☺

yo beauty here you are, and in your eyes shines the night time stars
and it's the blessing to me your grace flows throughout your hair, and in return such warmth of beauty comes; in my breath by breath air
☺☺=☺

as your heart beats each beat, that majestic rhythm's comfort to me
this glee shall last for all of days, which gives me fire, to with you always play
☺☺=☺

here we are and as time passes our connection furthers love's journey, and this is our guarantee
such the secure lock shall be our holding, and my hold in you is my promising
☺☺=☺

meaning with I you shall never be left in dust, but instead, always number one
and sweetie I'm always ready and willing; therefore you never have to tug, which means I shall always give kiss and hug
☺☺=☺

I know our bond's always going to be, and is reason for one another we each have the keys
to sum it up your inside and out your stunning self-causes there to be no one else to choose, and has me, for you=the must
☺☺=☺

has it yet been caught, you sexy gem are remarkably special

along with that, it's your cute giggles and adorable smiles which brings I double
☺☺=☺
more than enough is meant and what your beautiful face always causes
which is reason cas you, you special blessing are always pluses after pluses
☺☺=☺
reason you such harmony romances my heart
and has you, you tender gift, above all other; as number one on my love chart
☺☺=☺

In the day lights beauty, your face has shines brighter than most possible
Such hold's reason it's you, I desire in my mold
This eye awakening joy, and glee peeps know of not
I promise stick with my love, and you not regret my touch
These happy jolts, happen to excite me
In and out of you is I, so tasty it is therefore it be guarantee you always need my tree
With your smiles, your cheeks light my heart
You can rely on and trust in me; therefore with those we begin our fulfilling start
In meaning my feelings for you, you so beautiful pearl have passion; for our forwarding

And it's my promise to you my blessing will never feel as I, you're missing
This is my guarantee, cas my touch shall always satisfy
In such the way, as the team our bond shall always see eye to eye
Baby girl my loving touch, for sure is in no disguise

Sit in my lap and just allow me to rub
For my caressing alone, shall have you feel that's more than enough
Just allow me, with comfort upon and within your heart; to romance
If you allow me, my touch shall have you never needing another chance
You are who I crave
For you I save
For only you and only in you is where my eggs belong
That sweetie, is my final song
Do you hear my tone, because it only plays music of your heart
Which is why there's no possible definition, that expresses my appreciation our relationship
long ago had the start

Here we are and it's you, who has my attention
By which means, between us there shall be no tension

Instead passionate rivers of Love have ground; as I dial into your beautiful eyes
So special and delicate those two are, that tender love's in no disguise
Therefore our harmony must be and shall have life-long hold
And it's my determination to bring our special times to shine like gold
We must connect and have mixture, and in such blessings there shall be no finish
Which's the guarantee, to bring you and I sweetie better than best win
Not trying to be to forward, but my feelings have only one mold
For it's that connection, which makes it for our relationship, I'm sold
You are it, with me there's not many; but only you are my tone
For this fire burns with constant hormones
And such harmonies for sure, never going to leave you alone
Truth to this feeling shall always, yes for eternal length be our trusting
And its reason, for each other we shall always be lusting
Happy hunger to touch, rub and feel, for you I have
It's this journey alone I for sure shall never pass
Which's reason I knew, it took, just one look at your ass

It's my romance and emotions; which shall have you always wanting more
Of me that is, for my guidance is for sure to have you feel that you're reaching the highest tower
And of my tickles, you're always going to want
Which shall have you feel, like not having any other font
It's this fire, I desire us to share
For with me, you can always rest in my soothing care
No greater than the other, but on the same page we are
Yes my dear sweetie that's you're reason my world, and therefore, for all of life higher than best
will proudly soar
This tickling takes on capital ground in such a pieced together covering
Our love has built such a blanket of peace and is reason to one another our hearts sing
Just how heart has shaped has me in an unknown land
And is why, for, to the farthest length in all directions, already my love expands
Such is why, for you to remain smiling through all of our journeys has me in complete awe
By which causes me, in amazement always feel on top

BETWEEN A COUPLE
WHAT LASTS IS FRIENDSHIP

As you smile, fulfilling flowers blossom
Which has me, in your direction come, come
Meaning it is bouts time, you let them shine
And baby girl, day by day to see and touch you, is mission of mine
Therefore as the team or two as one our connection shall begin
And to have you as mine, is the win
Such victory, has bright shining beauty
Which has me know, as the seed apples shall fall from our tree
In meaning hand to hand, and lips on lips, with trust of each other we shall form the bond
And such lock, other than ours there shall not be any other, as or thought
In this assuring hold is where our ongoing passion produces greens
That producing feed, is what shall have you know, it's on I you can always lean

I stream my hands, throughout your hair
In doing so, is the perfume of your care
Such, such beautiful symphony you are
For it be you, my dear sweetheart, who has my heart
And my delicate love, with such passion my emotions hunger for more and more of your touch
It's that gift; of which I can never get enough
Reason be your lips, hands, cheeks and breasts are such fine, fine candy
In which I yearn or long to always have such delicacy
Therefore, it's you, yes with you my sweet peach I desire to hold
Therefore, baby girl: for you I'm sold

happiness is what I desire us to feel, for it's true our kiss and hug delivers the seal
it's that alone which brings flavor, this supply is like no other
not tomorrow or any other upcoming day, it's now, 'I love you,' I proudly say
so proud is reason bond of I & you, this romance leaves no possibility to confuse
obvious it is, your lips I hunger to kiss
and the rose your body is excites me, which is why you girl must, must see
it's true as you speak that Love within furthers, and has me know we must be together
yes my peach it's your character which excites me, and is for us just one seed
these plantations pour from our spirits, which guarantees our relationship shall have no limit

and of course, crawl before you walk, which is reason awaiting your presence, tick tock, tick tock
I watch the clock
I just know that day is soon to be, for us to share is the gift indeed
now not wanting to be forever, but you must reply therefore hand by hand we can be together
meaning my dear flower, I never desire any other

I knew the moment you were seen, you must be my conjoining
Which's reason my giddiness to more and more feel, this shall at that time have me kneel
You read right sexy and there's only one for me, with you I desire more than one apple, falls
from our tree
This majestic blessing has such harmony, which leaves there no question of mystery
Simple it is my feelings have uprooting, which means there need not be any more confusing
Love, happiness, enjoyment, rays of fun, holding hugs belong to myself
These blessings have source of yourself
Such light has support of I
Ands reason, we see eye to eye

Reason be I see you, smiles blossom
In your caring spark, showers rocketing fun
Because I know, in your special self, myself has comfort
This genuine truth shines in every word
Your love of peace and innocence delivers such satisfaction
Those just read words, you must hear, trust and listen
Listen to that what you must know
Which is, in step by step process I desire for us to embrace, hold, feel and in forward motion;
go, go, go
While we hold hands such steps why I realize more and more the gracious blessing's you
Which is why I desire yourself, like the naughty animal, upon I sexually abuse

And that be my promise to you, which's because sweetie my gift, you I choose
Which stands as reason and solo meaning, that only you alone are reason my dearest feelings sing
That has purpose of being, it's your silkiness that overflows my heart; with passionate fulfilling
Which is reason our holding hands, shall always have the life-long stand
As I take each breath, and love's beautiful color has me thankful you I kept
This majestic harmony has me, more and more give thanks, knowing you are my key

as you breathe, roses blossom
just seeing your pretty face, is so much fun

such positive light you shine
and is why I have thanks, you're mine
nobody else has my desire
meaning uplifting drive occurs in I, because of your fire
that passion has us, for each other in forwarding process use
and my dear naughty, in the bedroom I desire upon self, sexually you abuse

my choice does come at once, but I just know my choosing has no foolishness
that wisdom has me know your body and face is no mess
and this has grounds, which is reason to me your smile alone brings the sweetest bliss
also it's reasoned our togetherness means you shall never miss
that right there my Lovely blessing, with gear to please I shall always better
it's because our love gets stronger and stronger
such entirety of romance does keep us together
reason be who we are, this joining shall last forever

Always on your side, it's the guarantee
Hand to hand, lips on lips our connection shall run long like the Red sea
It's just your breath, which my dear sweetie causes me to have the day of satisfaction
And blessing it is, our lock be so strong, we my precious shall never have any tension
It's that lock, all by itself which causes me to have relaxation
Therefore, has me more and more fall in love; section by section
These beyond beautiful flowers fuel my fire
That key alone shall make you always feel higher and higher
Such fulfilling smiles form, throughout our relationship
Longing to always feel and taste, delivers drive to intensify our friendship

I CANNOT EXPLAIN

Our nuts and bolts, have delicate form
In result, guarantees you with me, shall feel no harm
It's this piecing together, that's the hold of our forming
Yes my precious, if not yet you shall see our destiny of one another; in hands we are holding
Such tickling romance this is, which has result of love
In love there are no mysteries, due to bouts all other you shall be put above
Which has reason, your harmony of fire
That warmth all by itself, has me being your only buyer
Meaning for you, all the riches, all world's expenses have no ground to stand by your specialness
My best of all blessings, it's you alone who causes the sweet finish
Do you yet grasp onto concept, reason be you at my side I shall always have fulfillment
Oh yes it's true my incredible loving touch, you and I are meant
We have mean to keep and hold
It's that girl, which has me sold
For you I'm forever hungry property
This lock's why I'm never going to be the lean
My feelings for you are permanent
Day in and day out, from my heart to yours love got sent
Now my precious sweetie I'm ready to claim you as mine
Reason be I don't want another find
What we have, so strong we shall never state, we had
There are times of giddiness which has I just know, it's you and you alone
No other has possibility to fill that circle, another beauty like you is impossible

You're like the moon, so bright and shiny has I know our growth's soon
Like the ocean colors, your eyes shine bright like no other
As the flowers blossom in such delicacy your laughter tickles, and in such romance, upon you
my whispers cuddle
It's as the wildfire burns, uncontrollably you and I are two who shall churn
Therefore our mixture shall produce riches, and that's our division
It begins with addition, then sums out in multiplication
But it's you plus I, with mix of our love the product is many
Or greens uprooting, from there beginning
Your nest is the soil and my inner beings are the seed, and our life continuing is our destiny
It's in that truth I live off of, and is guaranteed to always see you as the hungered must

Harness me for I have you, which leaves myself wanting only you
Treat you are, for I desire to constantly eat your fruit

Yes girl your face glows and your heart shines, and it's those I desire to always claim as mine
For it's in two where your true beauty is beaming, and why I desire you to claim, on you baby
I'm always depending
In every heartbeat for sight of you I hunger, as breaths are in and out, it be you I long for
With your smiles your giddiness supplies, fills my inner self with fruits and food of loving kind
Such passing fulfills my being, and why when I see you I'm never passing
Because of you joy always has presence, and causes me to know, you make much sense

Within my heart and mind you're always blossoming, and it's that birth which causes constant
uplifting
These floods of glee, always have I see
Have constant joyful thrills, and reason's your presence always fills

You pretty princess, for you alone I'm always listening
And much more than one or two have attempted to have a beginning
But girl it's my promise to always have you and you alone
In my mind, in my heart it's the guarantee to have you, always withhold the home
Our home within one another there's lasting promise; which does cause blessings
Like no other that is, and that causes me to endlessly sing
These jewels have the outpouring of ongoing kisses and hugs
Meaning in result stronger and stronger is hold of our bond
As we touch and in return connect, in meaning our everlasting love shines joy
Such happiness results in us having an unbreakable toy
This is cas, like children our lock has the kind, gentle, caring and pure touch
Which means I know with you, better than the best there is such
That giggly playfulness carries us, to seeing the beauty in one another
Not allowing any distractions, our childlike acceptance pushes us further and further
In meaning you & I, such delicate art, have colors of the lif-long tie
Within and all over I is decorations of you; no other kind
You my pretty fire, which began birth with sight
And all over your face, I saw such light
It's that promise which does bring me fulfillment, and always causes comfort
Therefore, yes my beauty it be you who's my art
And causes me to always, in your direction move towards
And shall above all the rest, have the beyond highest score

Therefore I'm always happy & it's simple, which is reason I have you and you have me
Honored I am because you've gave me opportunity, to further into couple
And of course, we made double into single

Life from your body, does please, your sexy tease
Due to your cheer, immense blessings are
Yes my special blessing your half is that missing portion, to bring you in I, causes my desire to rub you with lotions
Which does, and always shall carry us further, for it's that guarantee which shall make me able to never say, I miss her
It's your touch I long for, thankful I am your hugs and kisses are never sour
Your lips soothe, and mesmerize, and your touch, dear sweetie I desire to be my punch
So, so fine and sexy you are, so gleaming you can be seen east, west, south and north
I can see our future burning bright, reason be our one on one light
These fluids have such the mixture of forwarding, in meaning the stronger lock is our teaming
This combination is our unbreakable hold, and is what ties together our stronger than rock solid goal

This fastening shall hold us together forever, meaning other than you my dear I not want any other
From the talks we had, these feelings have me know I'm your man
Which means you must be my woman, and reason's other than you I want to taste no other one
Therefore I know it must be only you, because there's no other woman I desire to choose
That being expressed is why I know it's you who I love, it's you my dear sweetie who shines the beauty, and innocence of the dove
Your beauty surpasses the highest expectations, and why you're my final pension
Therefore, it's now easy to comprehend, the one reason I live, is to be your property, because you as my owner is my feed
Such the lock and key shall always keep us together, and we so strong troubles cannot bother
In our peace there is our lifelong security, which is our heart-to-heart breath by breath done blossomed seed
It's now and always I'm proud to claim, for you I have nothing but love, so powerful to all problems it shoves
And clears the path for you and I, such the opening is beginning of our life long lasting ride
So girl feel my flavor, because like there not be any other
You as my girl, for all time you be the one and only answer, no exceptions, if, ands, or buts; which is why to you baby I must get closer
There're no times of not knowing, reason be together our hearts are sowing

So beautiful you are by yourself, and hunger you join self
Your smile brightens my day, knowing you are my only possible babe
And locking it is, as our relationship builds, your body be so monumental
Covering that note brings the table of frisky and flashy flavor, which has, and still does deliver
fruits that never leave me alone
My sexy I'm not letting you go, and never sampling any other show
You baby be it, and that statement be my promise
Now that you have felt my homie flavor, it's time I feed another shower
This fruit shall comfort, tease, relax and massage, just enjoy as my feelings kiss and hug
Open girl cas my delicate peach, your stunning beauty knocks me off feet
To get up I use fuel, of my passion for you, it be true such juice leaves I with final sum, of you

Ongoing warmth caresses hearts of I and you, this drive delivers us as only one another to choose
Dear rest on me and I on you, therefore as one we shall not lose
Minute by minute time passes by, while doing so, my kisses are to and throughout your heart
and mind
Please, please my sexy lullaby fire your love has devoured me, and such leaves know it's you who
must hold my hearts keys

AND WHILE WE LIE

Such fun I have knowing you cause, you assist me in forgetting all lose
To kiss you is the ultimate blessing, and my dear darling it is you who completes me
Much, much beyond beautiful cheer you bring to us, you know your sexy being shall never be
left behind in dust
That truth brings me comforting glee, and has I know is the beginning to our long, long lasting
tree
Has it yet been caught; you girl is all I want
Due to your friendly sparks I have no desire for any other, which has me know, like you there,
just cannot be another
My feelings for you, have glorious blossom
Which is reason there's ongoing love for you, my genuine jewel
In one each other's arms we join
To see your fulfillment develops, glorious coins
To hold, to hug, to kiss and to rub juice deep within I cannot wait
Such excitement I have, just waiting for that day
And woman I adore in my heart and eyes, you are ALWAYS number one
But keeping you all throughout me, is the guarantee to have life time lasting fun
Cas of our lock I choose it's you who be it
And because of your character, these happy times reach no limit

Cas of you no limitation to my enjoyment, delight, satisfaction and fire it's you who I know I
shall never miss
Therefore, for me there shall be no limits to satisfaction I dish out
Which has I for life lasting extension, cause I to sing out loud

It's in the wind, where I feel your precious breath
And that my lovely peach, of you I can never get enough
It's my goal to romance and spoil you all over
You are the hottie, I must move towards
Because it's true, of you I desire to feed
Just know it's on me, you can always lean
do you see, you have my loyalty
to be faithful, and live out honesty, which all as one defines me
always be on your side, making sure by end of each night we see eye to eye
such glorious waters color you, and it's that sparkle which has me know it's you I choose

this decision has the stamp on my spirit, which has root from my heart, and leads to us having no limit

that's where I always want our love, cas of your bouts all others I always feel above

reason be of you I can never get enough, for you, from my heart, outpouring feelings is my touch

and it's simple reason of that which burns in me, as we hug and kiss this intense fire has constant increase

cas of you I never be the same, such truth has hold because when you were seen I came

to your side that is, and baby girl it's my promise, all days you have my kiss

which has reason your heart and mind is my fuel, and day by day to enjoy happiness I use you as my tool

such food has awesome flavor, and it I do savor

meaning baby it's you and you alone who's delicious, yes girl each sweet and sexy breath be so innocent

it is that alone which has ground in me, and reason you must know there's truth to fact=on my shoulder you can, always lean

Reason our bond, it's simple for us to trust, that alone you to I, I to you unquestioning must be us

My dear baby it's you I love, and causes to all others just shove

Just look in the mirror, obvious is that amazing beauty of love, which causes friendships gear

To the right, to the left, below and above, for it is your light which caused me to come

For I such glee you cause, and gift you are is my life long plus

My dear baby you are woman I give me everything to, for that's reason between one another I hunger to use

Because now we hold each other closer and closer

And I love you today, tomorrow and all days after

This has reason, because our grounds surpass my understanding

This place, has us together standing

Here we are, hand holding hand

It's like the deserts, my love desires to cover you like the sand

In this intermixing, what we can make has no limit

Our combo has myself know, for that one, there's no other choice because you are it

Our love, beauty, trust and secure hold is our premise

Heart to heart, kiss to kiss, mind to mind, hand to hand and my surety in you, stands as my promise

Such flooding of our beauty, has the victorious finish

Yes sweetie reason be my erupting feelings, thoughts of, and love for you shall not vanish

You my dear, in my mind has lifetime lasting
And that's reason, it's you I shall never be passing
Which now, and for all time's non-ending bliss
Do you yet comprehend, it's you who always brings me never ending happiness
Therefore, knowing you tickles my inner self
And has me hunger more and more for yourself
The token you are is that guarantee
For that beautiful light in your eyes. and smile has brought me to see
As the product lifelong living is our tie
Beauty it be, our bond shall not have any tangling or bind

It is this reason which carries us to upcoming days
And pushes aside all that waste
Therefore, it is now, I look deep within
I try so hard, because it's you I desire to never be missing
Which has reason because just look at you're in and out, all around beauty
In meaning for you I push for more and reason stands as, as two in one I desire us to see
Here and now, meaning time is in present by which means there is no end to ending time to me
claiming, I love you
This key keeps our hearts together
So secure, which has formed from our love has lasting of forever
Therefore, for you I bend over backwards
Which is reason I long and desire to always taste you're in between custard
Such harmony tastes so delicious
This is cas your beyond beautiful life, my precious
In meaning without you, causes depression
Meaning my thoughts of you, have one mission
When I see my goal, there's happy times
Just knowing you my babe, does settle my mind
That alone causes ease
Which develops, as bright shining peace
And once seen following your bright shining smiles, beauty beats from your heart
Before now, meaning in beginning that light had been my drive to start
Such refreshment shall always keep our lock together
Yes dear what we have, has brought I to all others not having any bother
In meaning it be here and now I desire us to be one
Just stick with me, and I make sure you and I have phenomenal fun
To the extreme that is

And this has the topping, of my hug and kiss
In the repeat pattern, our lips shall connect
Such beauty is our lock, because to all it brings astonishment

It's now and for all life, for you alone doors to my heart are open
And once in, leaving is never getting my permission
Reason cas us stands as one, and you and I shall never be known as two
It's that fire which had birth of our love that's going to always have us not choose another
I do make it my goal to always flood you with all sorts of blessings
On those words, I'm not messing
This birth is life long
And from mine to your heart, is my song
Loose hunger of you, I cannot
Day by day, night by night you my precious are within each thought
When your face lights my mind, upon mine smiles blossom
It's my desire for you to willingly rearrange, and within my heart, move in
Which is cas, just knowing you has already lit that fire
Such heat withholds joy that always lifts me higher and higher
Meaning my dear sweetie it's with you, and you alone my intense passion burns
All by itself that fury shall always have me desire to, with you churn
And sweetie, with this mixture I desire you more and more
My precious, doing for you shall never be the chore
Such producing means doing for you always provides endless honey
Which the fruits lovely taste is much, much more than plenty
It's within I for you and your gentle touch happiness flourishes
That feel all by itself has I enjoy non-stop riches
All words of relationships blessings have sum of you
And it's those fruits which has me know your woman I long for and choose
To touch, kiss, hug, feel and embrace you is my day-by-day drive
It's within my heart love and emotions for you build; as if it's honey in the hive
In meaning to not have, smooch, cuddle and tickle I don't desire to comprehend
Reason already for yours, my heart has been sent
So my pretty pearl therefore I have passion for your heart
It be you my dear who's my joy filling fuel; of my day by day start
Here we are, and so kind's your smiles of glee
And it's that gift of you, which amazes me

Yes, cheerful spark, it's you and you alone who has me in awe
That light you are is key reason within my heart door is always open for ya
For only you, stamp, seal and deliver
Waiting for you, and not any other
Yes girl it's you alone, who has me
Which has me on you, day by day feed
Reason be my love for you always supplies uplifting emotions
For precious dear I've learnt from you friendly love; as the lesson
Do you yet see, it's you, you pretty pearl who has my attention
And for you alone, love's my collection
Like gorgeous diamonds, your beautiful smiles shine
It brings me joy knowing I can claim, you're mine
Bright light shines from your heart, as if it's ocean of gems
Girl, it cannot be put into words the appreciation I have knowing I can claim, you're my friend

OUR SPICE STILL SPARKS A FIRE

In such comforting ease, just knowing you pleases me
And it's for that reason, ahead of time I can see our tree
I desire to within you, supply seeds
Because your birthing shall color with its rainbow of beads
As this blossom takes place, throughout your entire body our bloodline is one
It's within only you, resting destination of my cum
Sweet, sweet and sexy your body's what I desire my life to form within
Reason be, because I have you I always have a victorious finish
With such accomplishment, waves of bountiful gifts flood I
Munificently is the colorful tickling, which has us seeing eye to eye
You to I and I to you, there's love blanketing
Therefore my dear, it's you who is my coding
Because just know, to always be your only I'm about it
And girl you be it, which is my pleasing sentiment
Which means I'm not going to stop until we're one; as our finish
All by yourself, it's you who's my varnish

Hugs and kisses of such passion, is our never-ending limit
My goals to have you as my friend, for life long ticket
While I look at you, my smiles develop
Forwarding, is our promising relationship
This cozy ease takes me to lands of delight and pleasing emotions
Which brings me know, of that it's you who has my hearts combination
Meaning your names across my heart
Therefore, it's yours, when you're ready to start

In what we are, such rich passionate love streams between our hold
And this fine delicacy, strengthens our mold
Which pours out, from our heartbeats
Reason be your in and out grace, it's your gentle love I just must keep
And it be these feathers, which tickle I
Melting in your inner shape, causes me to cry
For I know it's in that, where I desire to stay
It's in your arms, I crave to always lay
Listen sweetheart, our love is dancing

And reason our kisses, its colors are so fancy
Because of that, our party of tender hugs, romance our hearts
It be that my love, which has I never deny our start
In the night sky you shall always shine
Dear sweetheart your face, your body be so fine=☺
That's just what comes to eye
Because within, reason your life such rare beauty you display
Which causes unique fragrance and tasty flavors
You babe, I always hunger to devour
While tasting your sweet lips, are songs from your knitted heart; which play the finest melody
It's that reason my love, I hunger for just sight of your quit bombastic and awfully profound beauty
For that reason my precious, within you I long to blossom my seeds
And sweet, sweet honey such symphony's my only reason I in and out love you, indeed
Precious blessing, please baby smile
Therefore, tulips and roses bloom; mile after mile
With that, the yellow sun shines bright
As time passes by comes the night
And loves strength in your heart is why such joy shines
And my dear, so, so thankful and reason I can always say, you're mine
Which is because such glee blossoms, throughout your every heartbeat
Therefore. light and tender kisses, of you comfort me, head to feet
This harmonizing melody has such passion, and so grabbing
Which keeps strength in our fastening
In return our solid, and unbreakable love has life long lasting
Smile my love, because it's guaranteed you I'm not passing
Is it yet understood by you, you shall never worry, to lose me
Meaning I'm the key which never leaves
And you are the fastening
Therefore, you and I girl never have re-opening
Which's because our unity shall never need another try
Strength of our combination, pushes away all tear forming cries
With such passion, delicately your sweetening eyes fill my heart with overflowing happiness
And your love causing glee, delivers fulfilling hugs and kisses
Our beauty, within you and I cause constant blossoming; of flowers
Then having hunger our hearts draw towards one another
It's been drawn out, for you my dear
Meaning I have passion for you far, and near

Which's because I hunger you to see the truth of beauty you are
Meaning beauty in your heart, and eyes shines bright from afar
Because my love I've found you, I'm the richest man to ever be
Such outpour's so cuddly
This hold has tender grace
Which was woven by our hearts lace
I promise to push forward
In doing so, abundant blessings we shall walk towards
Yours and I's approach shall blossom fruit; which's the guarantee to uplift us
Our rises hold, and this is secure in relationships promise
In such promising lock, lasting key is our honesty
And if so, just how do you know me=☺☺

as your so smooth skin meets my lips, my taste is sweet and sassy bliss
knowing you and I are together, has me not want any other
there, there are your waves of Love, which flood me with more than enough
when it comes to you taste and tell I do not, do not want to lose what I got
there is never enough of you I can enjoy, just use and abuse me as your sex toy
there is no lease, dive in cas you get all of me

Happiness is comfort of your soothing touch,
And my dear princess your beautiful feel is more than enough,
I am ready to drink, therefore use your juice and fill my cup,
It is visibly clear you my dear are the gift of Love,
It is my goal to unravel or unfold within your heart and spirit; such romance,
Which means your cozy comfort has you in my arms and brings us to enjoy the eternal dance,
Well my blessing in you there is more, more, yes more, more than enough for me,
Thing is for your touch and taste I am always hungry,
Pretty, such romantic fragrance is your feel,
Your joy is my joy; such the deal,

Here we are holding hands
As time ticks by, passing by is life's sand
But with our connection such passion erupts
You can guarantee, you I shall never ever pass up
And then it erupts that tick tock time has made its ground
With our innocence, peaceful harmony is our sound

Yo, yo check it you want beauty one only is to look in your heart
The reflection you see is why if not right by, I am always near
There is no possible explanation for the soothing touch you give
Which is reason in knowing you is my fuel to live

In the night, your face brightness puts the moon to shame
Such hold is reason it is you I desire in my mold
This eye awakening joy and glee, thankful I am to claim I got
I promise stick with my Love, and you not regret my touch
These happy jolts, happen to excite me
In and out of you is I, so tasty it is therefore it be guarantee you always need my tree

With time passing, more and more feelings for you take shape
Reason be these emotions have such comforting warmth, I know you are no mistake
Ongoing fire for me, cas of you always is
Your face is great rewarding, forever lasting bliss
And such the filling joy your words cause, surpasses any other possibility
Which is because my dear gift, it's to my heart you hold the key

Thanks to, https://images.unsplash.com/photo-1515871204537-49a5fe66a31f?ixid=MnwxMjA3fDB8M
HxwaG90by1wYWdlfHx8fGVufDB8fHx8&ixlib=rb-1.2.1&auto=format&fit=crop&w=674&q=80

Ongoing salute, from me you have
Which is cas our steel strong lock, holds us together
Meaning, there not be one situation that has ground to knock over our tower
In such unity, covering you to I and I to you our kisses shower
Such unbreakable warmth, shall keep us hand to hand forever
And always girl, has me proudly claim, I Love her

As we grow closer and closer, woven treasures between us do and shall always continue to blossom
Which is why with open arms I whisper, come my princess come
There must not be any pause; this has reason cas just to feel you I must
You know it, you beautiful blessing you are always the plus
And yes lollipop to lick and kiss you clean, I have in mind to do
That is my stronghold, and has you with me left to choose
It is true, true that there is no possible outcome of pain with me
With such surety, just know it is you I shall always see
Yes my Lovable peach, your sweet, sweet and sassy spunk I shall ALWAYS taste
Meaning girl within one another, our just right font shall last for all days
And such excitement I shall cause; as I touch
And as our relationship continues and our built promising fire furthers us

The thanks and appreciation I are going to ALWAYS have for you, cannot be put in words
This ground has reason, because of our beauty we are for sure always moving forward
This move we take part in, shall continue for eternity
Meaning as life is, forever I in you, forever you in me
This movement is our forwarding motion
Which is like me rubbing and caressing your body, with fulfilling lotion
This walk locks our links we have tied, which passes on in our continuous push for more and more secure hold
And it is with that token we form more; in our mold

Here baby girl, here we are and it's obvious: you're my gift
And you got it, you are my filling lift
Because it is your waves of joy, which bring me satisfaction
Meaning you plus I, is our joining addition
Such fulfilling times of your presence romance me, as I live
To sum it up, therefore blessing of your presence alone causes, from me to you, gifts I shall always give

know you so, so beautiful present always can rest yourself, in my lap
and with me, there not be any conflict; as if you are in the trap
but instead, you I shall caress with romance
which is going to always last
for being the best, you've surely surpassed
reason my devotion, as my only I will never need another chance
besides you I don't want any other
in my cold days, you bring relief as my summer
it is your warmth I desire to be held by
that fuel is what does and always will give me the richest high
and it is you baby, from, I will never hide
which is reason there's appreciation to self, that with you I try

WE'VE HAD OUR VALLEYS

It is true, just when you think that taste is complete, piling on are more and more blessings of me
This intense passion shall hold our Love together strong like the tree
Therefore together, not as two but one unit our bonding key unites our happiness
And this precisely perfect joy, is the guarantee between each other we shall not miss
Miss what?, our endless relationship, which holds us together
In the strongest lock possible, is what our bond feathers
Yes, between us is not rough and rocky, but cuddly wuddly
Which is reason why, our Love, for others is not hard to see

as the wind brushes your face, your adorable smile brings such beauty
in your heart lives my hunger to feed
these tokens shall bring us closer and closer together
now that you are seen, **find anyone else I do not bother**
such the blessing of so, so precious and adorable Love you are
because of your gentle grace, more and more shine those beyond beautiful stars
that grace so delicately flows all throughout your face
in this I clearly observe you're so delicately woven lace
and you see dear, it is you I swear who has my full attention
meeting your complete self is the final lesson
meaning with aim or intention to perfectly please you, I study day and night
and your body, mind, character and spirit I'm craving
and reason be you, there are your fulfilling sparkles; which never leave me bumming
instead causes fire, which has me always hopping
I am always on your side; which means me you never have to be finding
perfect gift is your glee and I am always coming
our bond's secure, because between us unbreakable Love's swinging

such tie there is between us
this hold we have is the number one plus
of you I cannot get enough
I have immense comfort, because our relationship is never tough
before you no one's above
and if peeps try, then I shove
oh, oh my precious rose it is my fire for you, which desires to explode
it is your touch alone, by which can unlock my code

it is us, and for one another we shall always bring plus after plus
and all distractions, having no care or allowing no interferences, by me are left in the dust
reason you pearl, it is now I see who my true choice has always been
with enchanting eyes your beautiful smiles, prevent side wandering and re-routing even though
there is much noise
which has me boldly know I am wise to claim you sweetie and you alone; as my toy

even in the dark, your beauty shines bright
your sparkling eyes deliver such light
the smile of beautiful fire, is what you have
peace in you, is for sure never leaving me sad
your skin is smooth like silk
I desire to drink your tasty milk
dance in your beauty, is what I desire to do
face of fragile innocence belongs to you
such tender skin of yours I desire to rub
thoughts of joy in me, which is reason I dwell on your joy delivering hugs
just holding and rubbing you is what I crave
dear this hunger shall satisfy me for all days

It's you my preciously pretty pearl, I'm 100% for sure not going to miss
but you must comprehend, the blessing just to see you, gives my eyes the kiss
such fragile innocence is within your beyond beautiful face
warmth of ease I withhold, which is reason your fiery light is my guide in life's maze
and this shines in your smile
for you I would travel planet distance miles
because of you princess, I have the top score
and loving you gift shall never be the chore
yes inch by inch, in present my kisses are sown on each priceless heartbeat of yours
to sum it up, you are the sweetest and finest; so adorably tender pearl
I am confidently for sure, your beautiful selves what shall ALWAYS have my heart
which is cas it is your character that brings me fulfilling comfort
upon my spirit and heart, so strong is you, it burns
that's cas my passionate sweet, sweet romance Loving you is always on mind
which leaves me not hungry for any other kind

here we are and as we grow closer my joy filling passion furthers
such fire of emotions, has your twinkle cover

wrap me of our promising future
therefore, reason be your fragile touch, of jewels I luster
which causes me, in such harmony to smile
and is why I programmed, when I want happiness, you I dial
sweetie not hormones but feelings I have for you, are so immense
and from what I see, you to be it, just makes sense
reason be beauty which you are has no definition
therefore my doors are open, for you to enter; which want you to fill the open section
which means it is vitally necessary, you feel me and jump on board
meaning you as I, I as you must be our final score

OUR LOVE CONQUERS

as the sun shines your smile brightens me
having one on one relationship with you inspires my drive to feed
with your each breath your unique positive cheer showers my spunk
oh yes dear I promise you, you and I shall always have intimate fun
I do see within your eyes angelic beauty shines
literally there is no possible explanation that explains my glee filling appreciation of knowing
you dear, are mine
this is cas upon you, day and night my heart pours my Love
which has you shine the beautiful innocence of a dove
and in this peace, great cheer shines in your every step
therefore is another reason, I have complete gratefulness it is you I kept
which is just one reason there is praise to you for that body
such the blessing is my Love for you; by which concludes me
that is not all, my feelings which have intention to romantically tease you
this is cas one on one time with you leaves me SO, SO happy; because it is your fire in me, and
these jolts leave me with knowing, forever it is you I choose

in our teamwork, our hands are locking
meaning never again, for the genuine man do you have to be looking
it is I, who always be there to lean on
the guarantee's, with me you're always going to be my one

to touch, hug and kiss your body is the best blessing; all on its own
for it is obvious fact you for me, me for you before time has been sown
and yes my pretty pearl I can see it is yourself I immensely hunger to caress and rub
just seeing you has me know, of you I can never get enough
because it is from your body the richest taste exists
there is for sure confidence in knowing it is you, you pretty peach I do not want to miss
this is cas your smiles alone romance my body and spirit
such cozy innocence has me know the everlasting glee you bring, has the reach of no limit

greatest gift you are
amazing is your friendliness, because it shines bright; just like those eye awakening stars
then there is your tender body
now that you gift feeds fruit; as if it is the tree

which provides the richest foods
and from that, most definitely=you I choose
as I lick your body, finessing and feeling your skin is beginning of meal
so round from breast to breast my hands rotate like wheels
point being made fulfillment I have with you
that pleasure has me know it is only you I use

Do you yet realize, only your body's my craving
Have you comprehended, for your heart I'm waiting
There's time for each occurrence, and no end to our lips locking
I in your body, and you in mine has such the settle score
And has me, of you crave more and more
There just can't be any end to our bliss
Because if so, I cannot live
And some say, you're far past attractive
But for me, just to be with you is my mission
You see sweetie, it perks my daily life in knowing you like I
With such flowers, has me thankful for you I tried
And my lovable peach, to fulfill and satisfy you I'll never quit
Which is why just know baby, it's on my lap you can sit

stars light the sky, and you brighten my heart
I'm ready to start, my dear be open there is no need for I to hide
☺=☺
just listen to the waters of my heart to mind, that lock is my guarantee
and precious it is simple to use my key, it withholds your character traits; which are so, so kind
☺=☺
just rest and hear, for my sound is easily comprehendible
to rub and massage you I am capable, fire to please you is my non-stop gear
☺=☺
in you is my passion, and you know both sections
so nice is our time cas it has no tension, your happy light gives me the lesson
☺=☺
as we hold one another, we intertwine and mix as always at link Lovers
as your heart beats I can claim it is Love I heard, such bond has me not want any other
☺=☺
there from your mouth pours that tasty score, and it is you, I am drawn towards
as you lay in my arms our bond brings us forward, your delicious body is always the A+ tour
☺=☺

your character is plus, plus; oh yes easy best plus, it is not tough cas gorgeous rose the gift is you

to sum it up your inside and out your stunning self-causes there to be no one else to choose, and is reason why, to enter; is the must

☺=☺

girl my lit-on fire feelings and my so intense emotions, have grip of me, and are not letting go

I am for sure, with hold of you I do not want to let go, it is you, just to see I would dive to the bottom of the ocean

☺=☺

visible facts are right; your body is sexy and tight

which causes my mind to have thoughts of you nude and yes, those are nice, blessing is these thoughts develop day and night

☺=☺

as life passes by our hold of one another is more solid, therefore in times of need our treasures of Love bring relief

our so pleasing walk has truth; not belief, meaning our joining increases my knowledge

☺=☺

smarts of that, that has romantic passion within me, and such hunger to give kisses and hugs

it is, yes it be fact you, you beautiful blessing are more than enough, and it is that which brings me to true beauty I see

☺=☺

you are the holder, and it not be possible for there to be another

To see you, brings me smiles

And your smiles beauty, runs wild; as if those sexy gestures are the Nile

☺=☺

As I saw you, what is in your facial joy I just must have

No questions about it, I refuse to pass

☺=☺

Such know and tie is present

It is, that I earnestly desire to always claim, you I kept

☺=☺

And pretty pearl, for it's me know you are it

Therefore, I comprehend it's you, I can't miss

☺=☺

Reason choices in life, just who, for that one several opportunities have been pushed aside

* I did refuse, and for me my hungers had been in no disguise*

☺=☺

Reason this is being brought to attention, my intention is to inform, one I desire

And I am not down with after some time swapping tires
☺=☺
My full throttle drives to have that lock with solo woman
You the solo woman, I desire to have life-long fun
☺=☺
For it is, reason be you I push for more
Just to see you, has me know you're the most beautiful score
☺=☺
It is in this rest, rest of seeing you, I have such peace
But more than sight I hunger for, to feel you is so, so neat
☺=☺
Neat might seem simple but look in the mirror and I might be understood
And the sight might break the giver; from what I see, it should
☺=☺
My point is, for me to grasp in complete I cannot figure out
Not feeling you, not able to have; at times has made me pout
☺=☺
I must know why I see what I do; reason I know my sight sees in you such promise
Surely no more time can pass, with me not knowing your bliss
☺=☺
Which is why, it be reason I'm all out of options
And why, in me I desire you to function
☺=☺
Between us, at right time intermix must have action
To bring your fine self-fulfillment, is my mission
☺=☺
So great you are, I shall try my hardest to explain
Beautiful it is, reason I just know our feelings for one another are the same
☺=☺
And baby, it be you my blessing, who is nothing but the best
With plenty of situations passed up and there's practical reason; but you, no more I shall miss
☺=☺
Therefore, this time of silence need not be, but blossoming, shall be times of fruit
Which has me 100% know you are be my final suit
☺=☺
You got it right girl, and furthering apples shall fall from our tree
That's reason you must know choosing I, is not the ill seed
☺=☺

But the promise to push forward
In doing so, your abundant blessings have me walk towards
☺=☺

Yours and I's approach shall bring upon tasty flavor; which is the guarantee to uplift us
Our rises hold, and this is secure in relationships promise
☺=☺

Which does and always shall hold us together
The richness in yours and my lock, shall provide little sisters and brothers
☺=☺

Our unity is the key to our tomorrows
And it's true, for our path to be clear all problems I shall mow
☺=☺

Such the happy winner I am and reason be you are my score
And it is, you are more than enough therefore I need no more
☺=☺

In such promising lock, our forever living key is our honesty
Which is why you can be confidently cheerful in knowing, you're relying on, and trusting in me
☺=☺

To you my blessing day by day, upon your cheeks my care's kissing
It's your sweet, preciously perfect mind and body, that's to me the better than best blessing
☺=☺

Such innocence there is in each word, which has me withhold the winning score
+This is reason all over you, Love, care, kindness and friendship my heart pours*
☺=☺

Just look my precious peach, reason you I reach the happiest peak
Therefore, my beautiful gem I do not seek
☺=☺

We must feel one another, therefore untangle the not knowing tie
In amazement, at just how you sweetie would give the honor to I
☺=☺

And it's such the blessing to have sight of you
You're in and out earth-shaking beauty, leaves me with not wanting anyone else to choose
☺=☺

Gift to me, when doing so I enjoy tickling of your heart; which of peace and Love, is brighter than bright
And your glistening smiles, bring comforting light
☺=☺

Meaning it's the guarantee who you are shall bring me happiness; for all days
And these times, is why by me I choose, not to push you away
☺=☺
Therefore there be no need for you to worry
Just trust and know on me, you can always lean
☺=☺
Day by day on each other we must reminisce
And dear pearl, this makes such sense
☺=☺
Heart to heart, spirit to spirit we have connection
It's true my heart, is the definition
☺=☺
It's yours, if you want
It's at your door, meaning there be no need to go for the long shot
☺=☺
Because it's when looking into your eyes, there dances childlike peace
Therefore, within these out flowing gifts, your Love comforts me
☺=☺
These decorative sparks color
Which leave me not wanting another
☺=☺
And I can see in your traits what you desire
Feeling of massages, which does fuel my fire
☺=☺
Meaning my sweetie pie you and I shall have endless fun
In other words within my arms come, come, come, come
☺=☺
Therefore, as the couple, for all time you and I are going to dance
That my precious and worth everything gift, I do not want to pass
☺=☺
You see my sweetly fine dear, in my eyes in my heart no other woman has ground
It's your pretty laugh which soothes due to its easing sound
☺=☺
With you I do realize how such eye gazing flowers blossom
Which means, of you always need more than just some
☺=☺
This is when your beautiful light shines, shines so bright
Which has brought and still brings me the one intention sight

☺=☺
That is it, always know you are it
Yes girl I want you to be my finish
☺=☺
As time passes by, for you who is pearl of my eye
My determination, until I get I shall always try
☺=☺
This hunger is feed by your glee filling character
And due to your innocent fire, having the gear of satisfaction sight of you alone has me always have the score
☺=☺
Your every heartbeat in the rain keeps me warm
It's our connection which always has the stronger and firmer form
☺=☺
Sweetie dear there's endless blessings, therefore for you I have driven to find and be door opener
Meaning hand by hand I want us to feel one another
☺=☺
You see my beautiful blessing, for it's you alone which has me continue to think and search
Until I find, which shall always take place I look for how I can burn you more and more; with my loving torch
☺=☺
So dear darling hold on and never let go
Our steps together shall form unity, which is our life long show
☺=☺
Sweet, sweet and sexy have you heard the gift above rest is you
In return leaves me with the sum of only you to choose
☺=☺
Therefore, the tickles of you color my heart and mind
Which has me know like your special self, there's no other kind
☺=☺
Meaning as the team, on forward I desire us to go, go, my diamond, let's go, go
Which means I, only have the font of one show
☺=☺

As life's ongoing journey continues its course, upon your face beauty takes birth
In such harmony, within your eyes pearls of such light play a role
And these duties grab attention of all, who pass by

You see my dear love, what romance your beauty causes
A melody of rhythmic peace, you're each beat delivers
This powerful, yet fragile key moves movement, within my heart
So baby, I'm ready to begin, meaning jump aboard and let's start

Within a mystery of ups and downs, our love remains solid ground
These journeys have brought us closer together, and lifted questions of doubt
Not between you and I, but foolish folk who refused our chance
Such times has opened our eyes, to special light each has
In questioned times, of unsettled past worrisome people have attempted downfall
But baby, that's where we stand strong
It's why our solid foundation, and our trust, lasts a love like no other

THEREFORE, WE ENJOY

Here we are, and I hear the bells ringing
Such a sound, causes the birds to be singing
Times like this are on of a kind, which is why with you the bountiful charm I feed, will always
draw invitations
And I'm not one to pass by an open opportunity
Seeing your hearts doors are open, wanting and needing more, draws me to your doorstep
It's currently which I realize, there's more of your heart's delicacies awaiting
Reason I'm always in need of you, I just can't pass up this opportunity
Therefore, for you dear I stand faithfully

Our love ties us together, meaning other than you I want no other
True is in your delicate eyes such passion burns, and within our hearts love furthers
It's simple to see, in you is me
And there's no disguise, you in I
As we live together there's our forever living candy, and reason our tree we have such fruitful surety
It's so obviously simple we've been made for each other

Pure and gentle emotions develop, between you and I
At night reason I have your marvelous love, peace is mine
It's during these times of joy, beauty fuels our tree, and it's those tokens which I feed
Grounds of your body I long to explore
Because hunger and thirst of you has me want more and more
Which is why, as yours I will always be happy
And why I just know precious fruit will fall from our tree

Through journeys we live our bond grows and patients strengthens
It's now clear, you're my hearts missing section
Within I roses blossom, as you breathe
Yes dear upon my spirit you're such a tease
For complete happiness, within my arms you can always lean
It's you babe I crave, and desire more of
And my sexy, of body I just can't get enough
I see your pretty face in the suns warming light
So fragile it be, and reason my sweetie's delicate peace, glee's mine
Your perky cheeks deliver graces loving touch

And babe, of body I hunger more, and much
Sweet and sassy's the loving innocence of your eyes
So obvious, such purity are smiles
Endless lively blossom's on speed dial
Hours and days we have are just ours
And my entire heart's only yours
It's in the unbreakable bond we have, our happiness furthers
And why in direction of the beating love I move towards
There's solid built kisses and hugs, in our genuine sword
And the gift of giving peace between us, keeps us together
My so, so blessed gift you cause immense harmony to have the hold
Hold of my heart, which is why in your purely delicate self I desire to be mold
Have your heard, and do you see our hearts have formed a limitless treasure, meaning all above
the rest fruit filled tree
It's in this hold our tickles grow, and our love shows we
This pitter patter of great joy, comforts as we lay
Which shall hold us together for times lasting days

There're such beaming jolts of blessed fire in our lake of love
It provides beauty and innocence of our love shining dove
This purity gives us endless warmth
And ties our bonding comfort
Sweet, sweet, yes my sweet and sexy, your body my lips crave
It's true, reason your touch I feel saved
From what, you ask from my depressing and lonely days
And I just know this fire of bliss, which has taken no phase
Then it must be true you were meant for me, me and I alone
It's obvious in your day by day loving, that beyond beautiful grace shows
Such the gift like no other
So delicious is your taste, for your juice tastes like the most delicious custard
Great tides of joy pass through your lips
Such comfort tickles, and blesses with a so tender kiss
A fragile touch, all to its own
Yes my sexy babe, only for I, I just know you've been sown

A peck of peace, and hugs of fragileness is your bliss
Gentle kindness blossoms within a kiss
Such fragments of pieced together purity

Do you yet realize, a stance of friendship is you and me
Our bond began long ago, the twists and turns we've been through amount to no other
But then like you're in me, I in you, and past one another we can't go any further
Baby keep smiling, because of you I will never lose eye
Reason be because of you I never have to find
You see sweet sexy for you there's always I
Yes peach that's right, it's guaranteed for life I'm on your side

There you be, immense tenderness, and unthinkable comfort
Yes sexy, it's only you who is my one and only treasure
Like you there's no other that I want
In beginning it didn't make sense, but I put in full effort, and went for the long shot
Present to me you are, and deserving of I'm not
But appreciative I got
Why you like me still has me
I still look forward to the day we fertilize our seeds
The greens we will provide, shall produce productive fruit
And such riches, will guarantee the endless loot
With the richness of beauty a loop or swirl of gifts shall cover
This amplitude of fulfillment, which has birthed from your womb will coat world with such color
My special blessing our tickle began in me, and built in you
Come before you I do, in awe of how unique is your heart
This realization has I giddy, so cheery I've been given the start
I just know our delivering warmth, shall bring us endless times of gentleness
Such care for one another, for sure shall further our oncoming with fragile bliss
These times of ongoing joy tickle tease, and such blessing has me always use
Which leaves me full throttle, towards only one I choose

A cute gift you are
With pink cheeks, and shiny eyes for sure you're my star
Like no other, you're way, way by far better than best
My dear princess, I have you so screw the rest
Lollipop of delicious flavor, a taste like you doesn't exist
So, so thankful I am, you I haven't missed

Waves of blush coat your heart, with a powder like no other
To touch or intermix with new pieces, I don't bother
Why such questions of truth you have, I just don't know

When girl, yes at what time did I show
What's up with such mystery
Throughout days passing, I give you all of me
Wanting you to have nothing but better than best
Not knowing I am, when I give entire effort, so in and out you're blessed
Why you have anger towards, still has me being dumbfounded
When for only you, I have built and founded, I'm needing to know why I'm being punished
There just must be an answer, to why such dispute
You look at me as if I like, when I only hunger to hold you
Yes peach in and out only your body I desire
Of its purely infinite beauty I shall never grow tired
Which is why to me it's a mystery for reason of myself you want no more of
Just what did I do, reason for such is, this battle of not knowing's so tough
Because I so, so desire to not lose you we must stop, communicate, listen and work it out
It is in our words, and feelings we will find or reach equal ground
And to one another, our hearts will sing such a rhythmic sound
So girl we need to stop this garbage of arguing and disputing
Then sweet candy, we will continue our bond, and to one another, full of glee we will begin
singing
Sweetie it is in these days such times of further carrying will begin
It's my goal, to please you so much when thinking of me for you to state, I desire only him
Therefore complete will I have to strengthen your fire, and harness your desires
And peach it's of those, I shall never grow tired
Meaning we both must put in whole hearts gear, and leave nothing behind
To do such art, teamwork must be our one mind
And there's not room to have any other flavor
There's only one for me, and your original taste, will never go sour
It has soothing fragrance never tasted or smelt
Once done, to my knees I just melt
You must know for I have nothing but positive emotions
Which is why, between us there need be no bickering, and connect in one motion
Such harmony will require effort, and that's where our deep within beauty goes past all
understanding
That bond we must find, which will carry us to above rest be surpassing
Such covenant of furthering, and agreeing grounds will bring us to exceeding
Reaching exceptional times will guarantee us, in and out happiness
For such to take place, we must stop our own desires, and to one another live out our promises
These words of truth need to act

In a mystifying lock such ongoing words of truth will begin our connection
It is in these times such romantic pleasure shall tickle you and I
Yes dear rhythm of peace between our lifelong ticket of hand to hand guarantee
Meaning baby, it's I you will always see
There's going to be room for no more
It's realized, because I have special love, winning score's no chore
Now I know, why there's the need and hunger to feel
And yes babe, our lock n love has a life-long seal

MY GIFTS ARE ENDLESS

Just open your eyes and look
Long ago, reason who you are my heart you took
As we sit and converse, such melody of peace plays
And there is the great need to hug, and kiss you
It's a no brainer, other than you my love there's nothing better to choose
Therefore I strive and attempt to do nothing but please
When I first saw, all better prepare to cease
For you I'd put up a fight
So honored and blessed, it's me who's in your sight
Which is why, there's been onlookers, but I had to direct them towards other kites
It hasn't been easy, but for my lollipop I expect nothing else
And it's true when naughty, I must unzip, and pull out my belt

Such rhythm of majestic love feathers our hearts as we embrace one another
To feel and taste you, is a blessing like no other
It's in this dance our connection colors
As time passes, more and more in your direction I move towards
For it's in the secure hold we formed, which paves our path
Such joy we formed, as our conjoining math
Within bonds lock our kisses and hugs seal the deal
And ours is a lasting, love-built meal
In our lasting security, the strong hold fastens
This gripping love has a tender but firm mission
Which is to gather our hugs, and kisses
That innocence dear shall always be our
These lasting goals maintain a key of guarantee
Happiness of such, leaves no chance of mystery
Piece by piece such warmth provides delicious fruits
A flavor like yours, upon my lips is so, so acute

Baby girl, you so, so sexy
Your shape just drives me crazy
Such tender circles, just comfort my hands
And your blessed kisses, have me as your #1 fan
To reach our purity, required is my touch, and your graceful love

Such beauty beats in your heart, as the beyond beautiful dove
And there my precious blessing, here it is your blessed innocence shines like a fire torched sun
So therefore baby, in and out our thorough mix contains It's this my sweetie, and reason your
touch of light such endless blessings constantly unravel
Yes my dear love, for just the sample of you, lifelong miles I would travel
You see my adorable love, it's only you I desire
And of your taste, and touch I shall never grow tired
Like you, my sexy gift there never has been, and will be
Which is why, within only you I desire to plant my seeds
Yes girl, you are it my final mission, and intended goal
Across my heart, your name's been written big and bold
For you, my fire burns life which comes near
Yes my dear forward, and as one's my gear
In each journey, as the team we'll complete all tasks
Towards one another, long ago we've taken off the masks
Reason our drive, and so sincere passion we have nothing hidden
For each other's touch and hold, we're always game to dip in
Meaning my sexy peach, lets begin sexual relations
It's true reason our emotions, and love we both have that mission
And so, so sweet and sassy love, your fine body, just has me down on my knees
Therefore, just to taste body, always girl I'm hungry

To taste and massage your body, such delights enjoyed just licking your pussy
Just know my dear love, you can always depend on me
My sweet love, rest your body in my arms
For girl no question about it you're my hearts charm
You're a gift from love, like you there is no other above
Your passion, and friendly charm, has tools of a beautiful dove

What you my peach, and I your protector have blossomed into, shines the most pleasing love
Towards each possibility, reason you, towards trash I hurry like shove
Do you yet comprehend, it's you who has my heart
And I'm in seat, buckled with your love, and ready to start
On whichever street you're on, my support's game to be leaned upon

Such a beyond beautiful gift, which always gives me the lift
Our journeys have paved our path, you and I together is blessed math
So unique and special you are, so close to me, in my eyes you're my golden star

A precious touch of love, to touch, hold, cuddle and kiss, it fuels my want to must
Therefore, my sweet baby, do you see it's I who's always before your knees
My pearl of beauty you're such a fabulous gift, and I'm so grateful you I kept
Like you there is no other, because besides you, there's not room for another

In the wind I can hear your heart, which confirms my keeping you, was smart
When our rough patches are, I smile because you my charm
Such tender kisses and gentle hugs, cause fragile innocence of you, the chosen one
So remarkably pieced together your life is, a profound mean of which I don't want to miss
Your smiles enchant me with peace and beauty, so, so sweet and full of grace your fruit is to my tree
Only for now it's my tree, and in time the tree will be one of you and me
There just has to be sense to you, each look I'm so taken your awakening beauty I'm left confused
There must be the way for me to inhale your ravisher looks, I tried on own and spirit and heart feel cooked
You see dear your astonishing grace tickles and teases, it's now I know the key's you, which pleases
Where can I look and not see your so delightful grace, and for sure baby, through your tongue, from your lips a sexy lace
It's you sweetie who has me in and out, so into each another you are leader and I am scout
My sweet peach I'm not like any other man, it's said he's above she, but for that I don't stand
Reason comes as you were made as my gift, and just to be with you is the best compliment
Therefore if ever you tired and need to rest, I'm here to be your nest
For you to lie and rest, which opens doors for me to sweep away the mess
Baby girl, you must understand, it's only you I choose, reason those other measly bystanders who've tried I let loose
It's you baby I desire to touch, yes dear of your body I can't get enough
My sweet and sexy blessing, for you daily I'm thanking
Your life is so, so special and unique, I just know there's no woman better than you to keep
Which is why, my special sweetie I long to cause smiles, and reason to feel your body on mine I would walk mile after mile
Sexy baby, our love has such glorious light, which erases all fights
Tender gift you are, so well put together, with beauty like no other
So my yummy blessing, your body is hungered for, which causes in your direction I move towards

Delightful gift, oh so beautiful gift, what the creative and tender love you are
In my heart, you my beautiful star
For your touch, I have the greatest hunger
And baby, there's no definable existence, to express my feelings for you; my treasure

Sweet and sexy, I have passion to rub and massage
From head to toe, making sure there's no section I dodge
Do you yet comprehend, you are my everything
Like you, there's no better blessing
Your innocence shines that of a beyond beautiful dove
Which develops the final grounds of our lifelong love
Has it yet been grasped, I strive to entirely please
Therefore I bring loves comfort, and cuddle your heart in graceful ease
Meaning my heart beats within yours, resulting in blissful candy as ours
A precise beauty shines within, and you babe, are my finish

The piece of art you define has a graceful touch of peace
And this harmony tickles and colors me
You see baby, it's love I desire and reason your mine, such treasure I got
Choice was mine, for you, to have patience, therefore there's ground which verifies for you I no longer sought
Therefore truth exists, which explains words or explanation has not been, which explains my feelings
Sour or lame, feelings of those has no right to be forming
Do you yet understand, I yearn to taste no other, except you
My special babe, now there is romance in us as me, or we as you

So naughty we can be
And hunny I can't wait, until fruit falls from our tree
Due to our teamwork, our growth has such firm ground
It is that, which delivers in and out the so, so sweet, and relaxing sound
So babe you never have to worry, because my shoulder will always be present to lean on
You bring me soothing and unique feelings day by day, night to dawn
You're one of a kind present
I sometimes feel as if from holy Hands, you've been sent
That and your beyond beautiful character's, why for you I'm always longing to satisfy
My lovely babe, do you comprehend it's only you I desire, therefore I don't want or need any other tries
And my love, for life I have intense passion for only your body and spirit
By which causes the lusting, of a hunger with grounds of no limit
Now babe we shall unite as one, or come together as one unit
Therefore happy times, shall reach grounds of no finish

In and out, your heart's what has myself glued to you
Your beautiful self leaves possibility, of there's no other to choose
With me girl, I try my hardest to not cause stress or depression
Reason to always have you, feel like A+ is my life long mission
And in me striving, it's my drive to embrace you with passionate sex
Within our connecting, the feel of firm hold lasts as we intermix
In this tickling rampage, a great force of friendship interlocks our bodies
With such togetherness, is our unbreakable, always lasting unity
Do you now see, as one we make the kick ass team

Tender love, you just must enjoy what we are
It's in my heart, and assists me in living out your card
You see babe, I've made my mind up what we have, just can't be lost
Even if babe it doesn't change, I want no other shots
I'm happy with you, the blessing I have
Our to and fro honesty, never leaves us feeling sad
For other times which are opposing we must put behind, and not look back
That means sweetie, I never leave you feeling like you have to pack
In doing so, a finesse of sassy and sexual tang shall spice up our low times
An easy feel of lasting fruit, will blossom in our find
Therefore you and I shall shed no more tears, or outbursts of aggression
Which guarantees our hold of friendly love; as our passion driven mission

These times of such troubling events, cause mystery in what's meant
We enjoy times of giddy joy, but then you disappear with leaving a sample of your toy
Your games of confusion must end, for I'm not one, left to right you can bend
What must happen, for times of hurt to stop, reason be I'm fed up to top

There's such sexy passion between you and I
To please and soothe, I would give try after try
These emotions I give, day by day
And still you push aside, claiming you want another lay
In order for you to see, what must I do
Because baby it's fact, only you I choose
For my entire life, it's guarantee I will live such truth
Which is why I'm dumbfounded on why, my endless love you don't want to use
My dear baby, you must comprehend it's only you I don't want to lose

For girl I would bend over backwards for just a kiss, and lose all senses in gear to have you on my side

So now sweetie for just one chance, to devote myself entirely in your grasp, I'm waiting in your hearts sight

Therefore, there need not be any more waiting

Because sweet cheeks, for yours my heart's singing

Meaning dear I'm here for the long shot

Your spirits golden ticket, I have bought

For it's been preordained, and our destiny's in one another

Meaning babe I in you, and you in leaves possibility for there to be no other

There's no other, uniquely special, and richly deserving like you

It's your in and out beauty, which has me be your prime target to use

As I sit in life, each breath's thought is about you

And it's with such time, my sweet passion leaves me with no doubts on who to sexually use

It's now my lullaby, for special design I surely want no one else

Which is because it's your heart, breasts, lips, and skin I've felt

Some days pass, and its minute by minute you I crave, which means, just for your feel I would wait all days

Do you yet comprehend, it's you baby day by day I hunger, which causes such continuous or ongoing fire

Therefore there need be, on day by day basis, your so satisfying taste,

It has such romance, and my heart it takes

Such delicate and precious love, for you I would and do give my everything

Baby dear, my precious love you are my everything, and to be better, there's no possibility for no one or nothing

I'm down on my knees confessing my whole hearts love, for my dear pearl your magnificently superb beauty brings to mind, the beyond beautiful innocence of a dove

YOU CAN TRUST ME

So sassy, and so yummy be your comfort and soothing touch
And upon I, it be more than enough
Such the bright star of love you are
And girl I be at your heart's door, always ready to more
Which means you are it for who I choose
So full of wonder, and grace, it be you I definitively don't want to lose
As time passes, we must stop missing the chances
And look past, even though our friendship dances
For us to further in one another, time after time there's the green light
It's time games are stopped, and as one, give full might

It's in your fire gear beauties high flying
Now sexy chick, here we are and as a team there be no more trying
So, darling shake that fine rear left to right
And sweet cheeks, are the prize always in sight
Therefore, my sexy spice your heart beats within my heart and mind
So unique and specially designed you are, for flavors and taste of your body be one of a kind
Now it be time to quit often taste, your soothing juice I yearn
Dear blessing, those bedroom lessons I desire to learn
Thing is, I only desire to taste and be with, therefore it is about being schooled
Which is why my beyond blessed gift, my heart only has room for one love
Sweet babe, all I do is give you my whole hearts love, and I desire no other man be put above
Because I've named you number one, I desire that in return
Sweetie pie, within one another I desire we churn
And with kissing and hugging, we shall feel such harmony
And it is current sexy fox is it for who I desire
Meaning it's my whole hearted promise to never treat you like a played-out tire
So girl, are you ready to let loose on our bedroom games
Because it be only you I desire, just you has my aim
But babe I surely don't like that game, and need you to stop with not knowing
Because sex of mine, I want us to work, and strive for you to begin showing

Because there's no rocks in us, is reason of one another we need not be absent
When you are treasured, there's curiosity on why you feel bent
Answers I strive or hunger to know

On why instead of yourself, you put on the show
What's the reason for your bewildering depression
Comprehend babe, to please and fasten with love's my mission
Only desire, to hold body, and kiss lips
Because sweetie my heart dances, just watching your hips
In your steps I see a rhythmic sway
And in just the feel, brings me ease as we lay
A beautiful juice I taste, from your body
It tickles me with romance, as we begin our tree
Such blessed fruit shall form in your womb
Such plans why we must stop fighting, and begin to use

Here we are, in such grace
And holding us together is such blessed lace
And as time continues going by, our love for one another is strengthening
It's now my so delicate and special love, grateful I am our love is no longer troubling
Baby we can now dance, and within doing so we form the stronger hold
For each other, and it's for that design, forms our unique mold
Finding such peace, isn't a easy climb
In doing so, awaiting I looked past several wine and dines

It's your heart and mind I've searched for
While doing so I passed some intriguing but shady stars
When you found, my length of searching not feel wore
Because, it's your specialty of love, which heals sores

I'm all in for you, tenderly unique, and sexy doll
When you are needy, I'm at your call
For you sexy cheeks, just know I'm in it to win it
For my heart you have, and for yours I have the ticket
There's only one chance you have with me, and you have long ago earned that key
It's not easy my delicate, and beautiful friend
But reason your genuine touch we have such the romantic blend
Baby as we hold one another, it's your body I long, and hunger
Girl you must grasp, I shall always be your lover
Day and night, I only desire your touch and feel
You as my woman, then wife for life, such the satisfying deal
Joyful I am, because you like and love me

So appreciative I am you have my desire; for us to build the family tree
It's in such lace, we shall build our finishing gear
And in doing so, as the team for one another we shall steer
You see my precious, it's simple because there's no more searching for us
Our teamwork has built the bridges, which delivered plus after plus
And now cheeks of beauty, there need not be anymore confusion
Because our difficulties have been solved with the confirming denomination
So tasty blessing we must embrace the love we have
This enjoyment need not go to waste, which is because it shall always last
Now girl of mine, it's time we stop playing slowly
Which means both saddle up, and carry on sexually
We need not let any more time pass up
For I'm all in, meaning desiring you drink my full cup

Thanks to, https://images.unsplash.com/photo-1619273328008-1a33a582f4e6?ixid=MnwxMjA3fDB8M HxwaG90by1wYWdlfHx8fGVufDB8fHx8&ixlib=rb-1.2.1&auto=format&fit=crop&w=667&q=80

Such the special meal you are, as a genuine blessing in disguise
Our hearts bod together, which is reason only you are mark for my eyes
And when the weathers stormy, our friendship remains strong
It's with you dear, our lock shall last all life long
Meaning there's no room for anymore doubt, because the unity we have outlasts every other
Therefore we must stop these childish games, and bring our hearts together
There need not be any more unsettle times, for our joy cannot survive, in such grounds
It's this mystery of brickwork, to each other's beat, causes a tragic sound
But sexy sweetie, it's now girl times must change, for the ongoing pattern of destruction must change
I'm not saying, it's all on you, because together we rebuild our bridge; day by day

My comprehension stands as meaning, it's you who deserves nothing but the best
Reason your day by day life, such evidence holds truth, and has me just know I have the win; in my nest
Already owner of my heart, and f
or you I would give my arms and legs
We shall always be, reason blossom of our eggs
Which are our genuine seeds of passionate Love
And that has me, about others always have you above
Such the blessing like no other you are
And in my heart, mind, eyes, and opinion you're easily the most beautiful star
Your smiles, and laugh, of love have a meaningful, and moving charge
Which has grounds of being upscale large
Being full of such comforting ease, your words sing in my heart
Which is why, about us there will be another start

❧ ❧ ❧ ❧

Happiness sounds such melody, for this gateway is home of our key
Lasting such truth, be our seed
Together as one we've built a bridge, and with such partnership there is to be massaging harmony
Now it's true, in this key, is growth our friendships unity
So fine and delicious baby, there are grounds of furthering roots
With our conjoining relationship, as a link for success step by step, towards all obstacles we are destined to bang, bang, shoot, shoot

It's in the present time, for you dear I would give my arm and leg
Our grounds shall always be, reason is our blossomed eggs
Therefore darling, we need be in no hurry, because right here and now my primal focus be you
Yes babe as the so beautiful cardinal, who is it for one I choose
Because you chose me, I have nothing less than high quality
Therefore is reason for loves fire wildly burning within me
With seeing you, smiles have stance, and in this music a rhythmic jolting fire outlasts
Which has me confidently know, you and I sexy will for life, will last
Meaning peach it's you, daily I hunger to insert
Or baby, for your touch me so horny, which is why when you arrive, I strap up, and rip off
your skirt
Not desiring anything except your sassy lips, tongue first I hunger to dive in
Having the earnest craving, there's not one step I want to skip

In our life's there's going to be journeys
Meaning, on one another we must rely and lean
Within us there's fun awaiting
Ready to fire, and have its lifting
As growth of our bond births, such treasures shine When such arrives, I just know you and I
shall have, endless fun
Our hold of one another, for sure to have lifelong last
Why I just know, you're better than the rest

Our hold of one another must, must not break, because promising is our wake
Our atmosphere provides such warmth, which has us towards one another come forth
As time passes our hugs and kisses have the tie, and this sweetie's in no disguise
As I taste you, myself likes the lollipop, therefore feelings increase
This sense brings my emotions, such ease
Our forever lasting love's where our beauty shines, which always has me at the table; ready to dine
Your body is my meal, your emotions I savor like the endless wheel
Wheel of water and flavor, you're the surety of never being sour

✿ ✿ ✿ ✿

such the perfect gift you are, it's easy to see you from afar
blessing, you shall always bring me fulfillment, ands reason for you I would travel that life-long mile
such passionate love's our locking bond, and shall keep us together, forever ever long
and with one another, the cuddly wuddly times will always be, so fulfilling equalities no mystery

in your eye's innocence, loves precious peace dances
reason you smile, your passionate and sexy joy lights the sky
with this you beautiful pearl, your precious breath soothes
it's so sweet, my spirit and heart get moved
which causes waterfalls of graceful hugs
in such romance, your fragile kisses massage my cheeks
what beauty you are, and upon I it tickles
oh my dear, blessing are your light and tender kisses
meaning you in my heart, you must always be confident in leaning on me
my beauty, reason our bonding lock, in being pleased I'm down on knees

**Thanks to, https://images.unsplash.com/photo-1607000975555-5e78c714dd1a?ixid=MnwxMjA3fDB8
MHxwaG90by1wYWdlfHx8fGVufDB8fHx8&ixlib=rb-1.2.1&auto=format&fit=crop&w=667&q=80**

Your body, I got hold of
Of you sweetie, I can't get enough
Day by day, I crave your body
Which is reason the more and more craving for you, has I needy
It pleases and betters me, to see, then touch and hug
Which is why, to lick and peer into your body I must
Why such emotions have had birth, has to be reason your special character
Such truth is because of your genuinely gorgeous core
The MOST gorgeous light, stems from your heart
And, has you at #1, on my chart

There can never be another better
Our love's the delicious dog, you're the ketchup and I'm the mustard
The treat our love shines, and with such the blessings unfold
Better we get in such the flavorful harmony
Such colors our foods shine, and such beauty isn't hard to see
Foods meaning the unbreakable bond which has united our festivities
Therefore, growth has blossomed throughout our activities
Such blossoming joy unites us together
Just know you can rely on me, as your sweater
To bring warmth at all times
The quiet times we experience are our showtimes

I'LL ALWAYS FIND A WAY

Here times are, with such questions
But just know you are it, because other than you there's not room for another
Why that is, has simple mean, you my beautiful pearl are meant for me
as your so smooth skin meets my lips, my taste is sweet and sassy bliss
knowing you and I are together, has me not want any other
there, there are your waves of love, which flood me with more than enough
when it comes to you, taste and tell I do not, don't want to lose what I got
there's never enough of you, for me to enjoy, just use and abuse me as your sex toy
there's no lease, dive in, which is reason, you get all of me

You dear are, free to choose
By us our proper love need be used, and should not be abused
We must study our choices, and determine what guidance is wise to use
Because our path, may lead to losing what's ours; to solve

My sweet and sexy pearl you must comprehend you're better than the best
Meaning your in and out beauty is far beyond all the rest
Yes, precious peach for you I would dive to the bottom of any sea or travel however many miles
In order to complete such, as fuel fire in your heartbeats are in my dial
Such a lock of endless beyond beauty we share
Look at or think of any other, I do not dare
Not reason there's fear of such innocence you have
But because when it comes to you, I'm entirely glad

My sweet and sexy far, far beyond beautiful blessing
There's no other better than you and about, for sure I'm not messing
To hold and tickle romances my heart
Your pussy soothes penis, which means with no other I don't want a start
And baby, it's you I hunger to hold and mix within my mold
There are such intense and massively strong uplifting emotions; which has me sold
Besides you, my heart has room for no more
Having sexual licks and kisses for more than you don't exist
And baby it's that fire I strive for
Also, why of you I'll never get bored
Do you yet comprehend I'll make sure we are always pleased

Along with life's pleasure, my special touch and love will always please you in bed
Meaning, you yummy pancake shall always be able to claim, 'I Love you,' my man lives and said

As days pass days my hearts colors, are remain on fire for you
Which delivers sum there's no other woman to choose
My eyes for you are so vividly in proper posture
From morning to night, I desire to taste and love no other color
So sweet lullaby you can know, I am the shoulder to lean on
And with only you, I so, so hunger to make daughters and sons
So, my sweet love, day in and day out it's only your tickling smiles I desire
Because in those blessings love unfolds and causes me thankful, I tried her
My taste has of your emotions continued my passion to have ongoing Love within
For you baby, and I'm positively sure your Love I'm never gonna be missin
And the gift you delivered to me, I hold onto and am sure to never let go
This birth has the ongoing show of tasty juices
Which travel from heart, lips, character and blessed emotions

With you I desire to make so many
And as such comes you and I will claim them as our victories
My special and sexy delight, with you I want to provides gifts better than any other
Therefore, my cum and your juice are prolonged in the flight for more and more
Which has you and I destined for ongoing happiness
Such has me know yours is never less, than the best

As time passes you and I, tickles between comfort our spirits
Reason we don't trust but know. there's no existence of one having a soul, our forwarding
growth has no limits
So now sweet baby. It's your call when you desire
Because my gear is of you, and that's why I never grow tired
Here we lye holding hands and lip to lip, I just know for there's only one score
That stands high and proud, as our Love solid tower

here we are, in such challenging times and through our journey we live teamwork which
conjoins us closer
it's those times when I embrace your heart and hold your lips within mine; which has me know I
got the premium score
on the mountains peak is my ego
your traits were my needed uprising, and now girl my class is on the grade A+ show

which has me know, better than you doesn't exist
just know there's no need to have, any type of list
because our in and out fire filled beauty embellishes our emotions
this passion ropes our mold, and has me know the steps we take will always have the same motion
with such rhythmic peace the everlasting bond we've built carries us as one
and in such music our blessed hugs and kisses secure our knitting
you wonder blessed by what; you see dear the love we have has carried our walk and pieced our
firm hugging

as I hold you, eruptions of harmonic sexy moisture tickle me inside and out
and that's right, just to feel has me shout
and this sweet passion run through my blood veins; which rooted in heart
that my love is the truth, which I base my life on, and it guarantees what got built will never harm
yes baby, through and through or in and out I belong to only you
and just know, reason our connection the love we built; I will always choose
forever lasting is my care and nurturing
and it's obvious, over you pretty peach I'm mesmerizing

because the connection we have is so strong, even when apart it feels as if we're holding on
there's times of sweet, sweet joy and favorable colors, which is why I want no other
these delicious tastes are one of a kind, to have complete pleasure all I do is wax that behind
nothing will ever be better; for as long as there's time, before us when I looked my eyes didn't find
not only your scrumptious body but who you are, and your one of a kind love is my golden star

as time passes reason our relationship, I continuously smile, and from such causes my heart to
beat wild like the Nile,
therefore, so much harmonic passions up rise, by which creates an overflow of joyful tides,
it's during these times I engulf the compassion you babe,
and such love from me to you will never leave me the same,
so, this means the rock we've built, will always cause arousal change

it is time to build our bond, and in doing so we will add life to our pond,
and so graciously beautiful it is, day in and out my vocals flourish, and for you I sing song
after song
when I sit, to dwell on my favorite blessing I just cannot have any other sum than you,
then there are times of joy that rush me, and I don't wonder why
it's all reason your smiles are a volcano of glee and every breath are twisters of beauty,
it's in that fury of happy blessings I smile high, high upon the mountain top

there's literally nothing, which can decrease me in any way,
for the font passion you cause to withhold any other than what your life shines I don't desire
and reason for such has no sensible cause but delivers such elite promises of fortune,
these riches dwell within your character, which is why I always strive blossom flowers in you
to just how my dear such were shaped, and how your beauty began still has me
I do understand one's lifestyle creates in and out beauty
But yours my dear has a flavor which has never been discussed or understood
so, either you're beginning isn't earth, or such remarkably fabulous beauty is the first,
it's never been heard therefore the large portion would assume the beginning
but I confidently know, limits do not exist therefore your hearts fires first steps were not on
the world

NOTHINGS TO MUCH

there you lie, as a pieced together gift
and baby your smiles lift, carry me higher than the sky
you're my one and only beyond blessing, and sweetie better than you doesn't exist
appreciation like no other I have, you I did not miss, for living without you is the route, which is
so troubling
such peace develops, while your kindness has a reflection of love
our relationship caused in our every beat the innocence of a dove, and its reason for our tender
touch we always overcome life's bumps
and under the sky we hold each other, I am so pleased your loves light brightens the galaxies
deepest distance
reason you I have found the sweetest gem, which will always cause me to hungers your lips, such
joy gives within the needed lift, the rise done through us will never need a trim
in our connection arises such blessed times, for during my sexy babe our friendship makes me cry
we're finally together as one, which is because we're connected as a team, we will defeat much
more than some, and sweet, sweet baby dear it's on me you can always lean
it's time my love you comprehend in full, these hurricanes of fire are for no one else but you
so, so special and delicate blessed touch of peace, besides you, my heart hungers no other, for
me such glee has caused such has caused magnanimous awakenings, my so appreciated touch of
love, it's you who is the best possible blessing, for that has me strive to be the right for you partner
to find and have you wasn't easy, but it's an achievement I will always be up most appreciative
you are it for who I hunger, and you'll always be first in line when it comes to choosing, and our
secret times bring sassy sweetening, which is why just to lick, then to taste your pussy causes an
outpouring of custard

there must be no end to what we have,
because such is from me and in your steps it's evident you sour
which has me know it's your tender love which causes an overflow of joy,
because of these uplifting jolts, the fire in me hungers for more
I crave your emotion causing bliss, that dear is the gift I never want to miss,
it's evident you my sexy plus were made for me
and my lullaby I look forward to the day fruit falls from our tree
times of flavor come and I hunger this infinite taste doesn't leave,
I've been one of intake, and you're so good I just can't get enough
From day one this wasn't hard to see,
there just be no end to you and I, baby just being your property gives me so much

the time has come, where it's time for you and I to make our lock more secure
we've outlasted our journeys, which were not tedious but did assure
these trials didn't cause our debark to be further
but instead brought our tie closer together
reason our hearts have been molded together, it's easy for us to hold on
and because we refuse to accept any side wandering thoughts, as one we shall always be on top

tick tock, tick tock, while time passes, we carry both, and in our sexual times of passionate fury
our love entangles within each
it's these occasions which tickle yours and mine heart, and feed our seeds
then the giddy joy we blossom furthers our hold, in a river of good times
it is the guarantee that your hearts waters of love soak me as though it's a delicious wine
baby, my doll of forwarding friendship you must understand I only want your heart
meaning sweetie pie, I'm in gear and so, so hunger you to desire the same start
my eyes only have you my preciously sexy flower as the forwarding seed
which means my tasty dessert you never have to worry, because I never try any obnoxious weed
therefore, there be no need to give any attention to side wonderin1g thought
because it's you alone I have caught

there is occasions of our emotional struggles
and during such is when we must remember it is communication which furthers the roots of
our cuddles
such are the times in which we hold one another in whirl winds of glee
and do you yet see, it's myself holding you, and you comforting me
as we embrace one another for who each is there be a massage of blessings within our friendship
this is when my lullaby we need to maintain our solid steel ship
it's built with grid thick love
and secured with kisses and hugs
such graceful security impresses all observe
at the wide variety of treasures
do you yet comprehend, better than you has no possibility of existing
it is all about your body I'm so lusting
meaning my love it be you alone who has my hunger for ongoing taste
and my sweetie this is for sure not any type of phase
this is my whole hearts love
and my sexy piece of pie it is your delicate beauty which shines the beyond beautiful innocence
of a dove

Michael Green

my cup cake of smooth and sassy cream, as I clean you it is mg embracing of such orgasms
which bring us closer together
during these times our so strong hold, toward each brings us closer
and such blossoms more and more of our love
my sexual obsession it is you alone who causes me to always feeling above

do you yet comprehend, there won't be another flavor that my tongue tastes
there's just no sense to missing for any number of days
because sweetie, without is what I never want to suffer
baby it's your sexy touch, which teases me with a delicious custard
it's not yet understood, just how a piece of art like you long ago wasn't discovered
because there's no possibility, it's not like with a more fabulous beauty you can be covered

reason your inner beauty finesses, and with such upon I my princesses heart blesses
it's like you feed me pieces of a faraway liquid, because myself yearns for what no one can claim
they did
I feel so unique, no one else like me, which is why I appreciate the two of us have grown from we
now babe the time has arose for me to again claim, reason you I'll never be the same
that means missing your touch must never be, which is because your mind, heart and character
have hold of me

with you dear myself feels complete
there's appreciation I'm the victor, ands reason I no longer compete
sexy blessing missing just a sliver unsettles
in my heart your loves bottled meaning you're the potion I'm the kettle

our love will always shine bright
that is, all day and night
such a faraway journey was not needed, but just the gears of determination and refusal to quit
reason our one on one relationship I just knew you were the right fit
because you're all I want and need, there's no desire to touch anymore
in meaning my love you are my final score

AS OUR MOLD STRENGTHENS

it's believed by some, as humans angels and spirits live
to experience, only one thing I give
to obtain rights, I don't need any permission
for me babe, to know such I don't need any lesson
because just knowing I'm without is the dramatic loss
and through dealing with such sorrow or anguish loving you comes with no cost
experiencing our favorable times extinguishes any chance of grief
baby, you're my golden star, in all of life's weeds
and I look forward to our tree, blossoming fancy fruits
reason our victorious stand, as the elders we will be used
your in and out beauty are the gears the hungry will yearn
for it's true my one and only care is for us to intertwine or as one churn
there just must be a reason the beauty like you wasn't crowned royalty
my dear love, you being my one and only I now clearly see

as time passes the tie, we've built secure builds strength
and in such treasured times we embrace one another
this is when we shape each other as one
our times of joy surpass all the off-scale grime
now's when our genuine mold takes its bold stance
meaning our loves outlasted, therefore either of us needs another chance

my love I've poured out my heart, and I'm well aware you're in it for the long shot
which is fuel to my gears and supplies us with tools to strengthen the lock
the security defeats all hardship to being trivial times
which gauren2tees as friends forever dear we shall drink the most glorious wine
it's in such a wonderful joyful praise I see and feel you
which shall always leave it that my only key is you

my only desire is to reminisce the shape and details of your character
that blossomed joy caused me to classify you as my golden star
in or through such the so, so craved times, as my true love I only see you
this hunger leaves me at you're the only one I choose
is it yet understood, in my eyes and heart you are my bright light

and even through our disagreements you remain the one and only beyond beautiful flower
who's in my sight
therefore, there need not be any more questions for who my one and only is
because my life's only hearts key equals the blossomed hearts flower
reason there's room for only one, you're the special gift I have won
I've poured out my heart, and am in gear for us to start

Sweetie, so sexy is your smooth and luscious skin
For sure dear, you don't need any type of trim
It is you my so desirable candy who always comes in first place
Adored gift the love I have's so strong I know this is not a phase
And baby, just know my arms are waiting for you to have rest, on any day
Beyond beautiful love you are my only intention
Meaning I always crave your gorgeous character, and thrive our relationship, which has no tension
That means my so, so innocent lullaby there need not be any more questioning
I trust you and you me; is my meaning

Such a journey of ups and downs, but sexy gift reason our mold within, conquers all possible
frowns
Desiring just you is very easy, which is because there's no other pleasure that blossoms ripe
greens
There just must be no end to what we have
Such confidence lives, because hunny just sight of you makes me giddier than glad
To always hold, hug. Kiss and make love to you is my life long plan

There are no words, which describe the desirable body and spunk you shine
So appreciative I am, that you're all mine
Where you're beauties from has no explanation
The phenomenal in and out light has no definition
Which means my adored love, better than never has or will exist
Even if you're compared, you'll conquer the list
Which is why my heart cries of appreciation, and of who you are my satisfaction's elated
And girl, even though there were many distractions you can confidently know, to all that junk
my love dismissed
Yes love, so precious and adorably sexy artwork you are, which means my dear you are my
beyond beautiful dove
Meaning baby you and you alone are it for who I love
And my so, so sexy and tender lovable teddy bear that is whole heartedly

In meaning sweet and luscious candy there is no other body and heart I crave

Therefore, reason your pieced together beats, by far amounts because of character you've assisted in eluding the depression and's why I can claim you are one who saves

Just the tiniest fragments of you, my ripe and lovable hunny for sure please me

And girl you better believe more than elite fruit's blossoming from our tree

With such majesty has me claim from within the greenest lands have sprouted

In meaning within us is an unbreakable lock, which is securely fastened

And that causes me to push and hunger to retrieve more of you

This my cradled love leaves with choice only you are only one for me, and it, for who I choose

As our unique lock strengthens, it pursues more lands of fruits and needs almost no assistance in doing so

The honey's fragrance tickles and comforts me to being who I desire, and reason our friendship that I know

So, baby I am game and ready to start, meaning hungering the bond we've built has a much, much more than strengthened wall

That means, having love all within being made with flawless beauty stamps the seal of us in meaning apart we shall never fall

Therefore, girl you and I will always be together

You as I and myself as you, who is my hearts golden star

We now have the connection which secures our bond

Within such a tie there lasts ongoing, for the untouchable connection; which is forever long

And with this I'll always see you as my beautiful and so sassy candy; which is so scrumptious

As my respectful and trustworthy princess, to me at all times you are the upmost courteous

Therefore, in my heart and eyes myself only sees you, in full focus

That means because you are only one I see, and that pure love who in my opinion is beauty who is just

Just for me that is and this my dear is what I sexually hunger

You being so special is what I surely luster

For my baby, it's in between your legs so, so tasteful is your custard

And always will, for it is the combination of unique connection that keeps us beating strong

This solid pace shall be forever long

Meaning sexy touch of love, it be your heart and spirit knitted with love, which keeps us strong

Therefore, we will never loose in all of our journeys

Because for each other's hearts we have the keys

In such passion rivers of love, we're carried together forever

Yes, my love for length time exists my love only beats for my cover

Which is reason my friendship fire curiously ventures from mine to your mind

This my blessing, just as our togetherness our love will last for all time
And blossoms our beautiful pedals of furthering and tokened flowers will always brightly shine
Even the smallest bit of better, it's not possible for me to ever find

Our fire-stricken teamwork furthers us as we grow together better and greater
Therefore, in our journeys our hearts will mold, as we will hold one another
Which surpasses easily greater than the best ever
That my love is my goal to make last past this life, which means our love will live forever

Here we are and with our every breath our heart intakes our as one lock surpasses any other
There must be some sense to that which holds us together forever
With such a superior friendship I just can't make sense to our so great and phenomenal
connection
Words or explanation don't have possibility of existing that explain my appreciation for how well
we function
It's true there not be any other light than you which has possibility of entering my heart
Which is why I'm thankful you were game to give me a start
Now baby buckle up and be ready for my get up and go full steam ahead ride
Therefore, in our love filled flames causes us to only have each other in sight
We will carry one another in our times of playful questions
You within myself and I in you is our mold and our hearts section
For these kind and journey filled times don't pass up our pivotal playfulness
And this blessedness caresses the combination of flavor and love, therefore our heart feeds the
superb creation of our bliss
Timeless is our ongoing love, which means we are holding one another in an everlasting hug
In doing so we will pass up all distractions, in meaning to retrieve our unity won't be tough

Your hugging hold keeps me hungry
And that need's why you shall always have me
To see you, brings me smiles
And your smiles beauty, runs wild; as if it is the Nile
As I saw and see you, what's in your eyes I just have to have
No questions about it, I refuse to pass
Such know and lock is present
It is, that I shall always claim I kept
And now pretty pearl, I just know you are it
Therefore, I comprehend it is you, I cannot miss
Reason be my choice of life, just who, for that one several opportunities have been pushed aside

For specific reason, I did refuse, and my wants were in disguise
Reason this is being brought to attention; my intention is to inform it is one I want
Such hunger arouses flames, of only one font
Your heart decorates pretty colors of pearls and diamonds
This precise awestruck beauty limited my time of mining
It's not only the impressive beauty of your glimmering face and fabulous body
But baby, those jolts of fire-stricken love, which entirely complete me
Our devoted commitment causes my heart to form tears of loyalty
Meaning besides you my sexy I want no other
Yes girl, only desired is that between custard
Now there will be no more flaws, which is the primal reason we've knitted the tie, shared those
words and have the unbreakable hold
Which means my pretty I can easily see I am for you and you were made for me
And now my so adorable and luscious babe, you're my key
That literally always makes me happy
Such fulfillment overflows my heart with glee
Yes sweet & sexy it does complete me

OUR BODIES
WEAVE WITHIN

Which is to have that lock with solo woman
With this woman, I desire to have life-long fun
For it is, reason be you I push for more
Just to see you, has me know you are the most beautiful score
Neat might seem simple but look in the mirror and I might be understood
And the sight might break the giver, from what I see, it should
My point is, for me to grasp in complete I cannot figure out
Not feeling you, at times my hunger has made me pout
All joking aside, I must know why I see what I do
Reason be I see in you such promise
It is for sure, known now is, no more time can pass with me not knowing your bliss
Which is why, it be reason I'm all out of options
And why, in need of you to spill; just how or why I need you to mention
here we are my love, and as our lips lock, our priceless relationship causes love to travel from
your heart to mine
friendship with an adorable angel is what I have and your taste is like a fancy wine
it's a delicacy to taste you, and not only your body has my like
check it, just to have a hug I would do an earth distance hike
who you are, I'm a fan of your beauty-stricken river which causes me to always keep you in sight
and as I drink from, the soothing custards, the massage be so kind
it is that my sweet lullaby, which I find comfort
my precious peach, it be your hold that causes me to always want more
grow tired of you, I will never
my sexy, there's no reason I will ever
with knowing you, it's not possible to be
as your emotions pour out, I engulf each
as the days pass myself looks forward to that time when we hold hands
for us to be one is my prolonged plan
in works is the process by which delivers greens
my shoulder will never be absent, for you to lean
connection we have are the greens, to our love's endless riches
in such are boundless fancies and limitless kisses
our friendship is the joy I live for

not having you is like an obnoxious sore
with knowing you, caused all the plaguing depression to leave
all those inconsequential feelings were seized
do you yet comprehend, at first you were a blessing in disguise
as time passes, I fully comprehend how fortunate I am you're mine

a beyond beautiful gift you are
from when you left mom own light surpassed the brightest stars
it's in these times my love for you overcomes all opposing distractions
its as if there's a force which wants us not to be
and this sweetie pie does not have any furthering seeds
therefore, my love it need not be anywhere mixed in our connection
and that my sexy doll, is the final lesson
final because our connection has conquered the rest
which means now my one and only we will kick it with the best

during those worrisome times, my promise is to always be there to lean on
I no longer have eyes for any other in the pond
There won't be anymore questionable times of me desiring any other
Because I whole heartedly realize you are my beyond beautiful summer
Which means I only hunger to feel warmth you shine
And my sexy lullaby I have you, which means I no longer need to search and find
As one we've overcome so much
And I will eat you for breakfast, dinner, snacks between and lunch

As we've lived as a couple, we've had enjoyable good times and it's that my teddy where we
complete goodness and flavored fruits
Therefore, I realize it's us as the rock-solid team is who we need to use
People do or will see us as a love strong unit, for it's that baby we must strengthen
Me as your life long love must be strong in your comprehension

Do you yet grasp onto my perception
I have seen your colors and do enjoy the pension
Has it yet been your understanding it's I who only desires you to have the best
To all others who I've heard are pretty; oh screw the rest
Because it's only your breasts and lips I yearn
You've blessed with such mystical flavors, which has caused me to learn
With such ease, as one you've carried me unto your light and tender character
Thing is if anyone asks who has the most beautiful, I proudly point and state, I have her

Thanks to, https://images.unsplash.com/photo-1607000975555-5e78c714dd1a?ixid=MnwxMjA3fDB8
MHxwaG90by1wYWdlfHx8fGVufDB8fHx8&ixlib=rb-1.2.1&auto=format&fit=crop&w=667&q=80

Day by day beauty uproots and blossoms wit Your hugging hold keeps me hungry
And that need's why you shall always have me
To see you, brings me smiles
And your smiles beauty, runs wild; as if it is the Nile
As I saw and see you, what's in your eyes I just have to have
No questions about it, I refuse to pass
Such know and lock is present
It is, that I shall always claim I kept
And now pretty pearl, I just know you are it
Therefore, I comprehend it is you, I cannot miss
Reason be my choice of life, just who, for that one several opportunities have been pushed aside
For specific reason, I did refuse, and my wants were in disguise
Reason this is being brought to attention; my intention is to inform it is one I want
Such hunger arouses flames, of only one font

Your heart decorates pretty colors of pearls and diamonds
This precise awestruck beauty limited my time of mining
It's not only the impressive beauty of your glimmering face and fabulous body
But baby, those jolts of fire-stricken love, which entirely complete me
Our devoted commitment causes my heart to form tears of loyalty
Meaning besides you my sexy I want no other
Yes girl, only desired is that between custard
Now there will be no more flaws, which is the primal reason we've knitted the tie, shared those words and have the unbreakable hold
Which means my pretty I can easily see I am for you and you were made for me
And now my so adorable and luscious babe, you're my key
That literally always makes me happy
Such fulfillment overflows my heart with glee
Yes sweet & sexy it does complete me

Which is to have that lock with solo woman
With this woman, I desire to have life-long fun
For it is, reason be you I push for more
Just to see you, has me know you are the most beautiful score
Neat might seem simple but look in the mirror and I might be understood
And the sight might break the giver, from what I see, it should
My point is, for me to grasp in complete I cannot figure out
Not feeling you, at times my hunger has made me pout
All joking aside, I must know why I see what I do
Reason be I see in you such promise
It is for sure, known now is, no more time can pass with me not knowing your bliss
Which is why, it be reason I'm all out of options
And why, in need of you to spill; just how or why I need you to mention
here we are my love, and as our lips lock, our priceless relationship causes love to travel from your heart to mine
friendship with an adorable angel is what I have and your taste is like a fancy wine
it's a delicacy to taste you, and not only your body has my like
check it, just to have a hug I would do an earth distance hike
who you are, I'm a fan of your beauty-stricken river which causes me to always keep you in sight
and as I drink from, the soothing custards, the massage be so kind
it is that my sweet lullaby, which I find comfort
my precious peach, it be your hold that causes me to always want more
grow tired of you, I will never

my sexy, there's no reason I will ever
with knowing you, it's not possible to be
as your emotions pour out, I engulf each
as the days pass myself looks forward to that time when we hold hands
for us to be one is my prolonged plan
in works is the process by which delivers greens
my shoulder will never be absent, for you to lean
connection we have are the greens, to our love's endless riches
in such are boundless fancies and limitless kisses
our friendship is the joy I live for
not having you is like an obnoxious sore
with knowing you, caused all the plaguing depression to leave
all those inconsequential feelings were seized
do you yet comprehend, at first you were a blessing in disguise
as time passed, I began to comprehend that someday you'll be mine

day by day your beauty increases
this growth occurs, as reason your life pleases
your heart, mind, body and spirit does so
which proves the extant of your fire has no limits, which to me is not oppose
I've put it in so many words and I want no other than you
the best craving is why it's you, I choose
I'm driven, by you day by day to be used
and sexually I have massive passion to be abused
with such leaves of varied colors my heart sings joyfully
it's that alone my sexy blessing that enchants me
is it understood that for me to embark a journey of step by step our hands need to remain
holding strong onto our love furthering key
and this gift will assist us in our promised treasures of fancy fragrances
our team doing and life filling or lifelong words to one another confirm our promises
in this desire has me hunger the most beautiful angel
my sexy lullaby your innocent beauty brings to mind a sun filling candle

it's with you that endlessly joy is felt
which is why in your bodies every fragment I melt
for that alone lives the urge for more
and causes us to always have the richest score
that high quantities reason together we're like a love-built tower

such ripeness we live develops a body that never goes sour
with such tides of love and fire fuel by the connection the one body we have furnaces the
development we shine
we're partnering friends, therefore not often is it yours or mine
instead, a partnership of relationship and laughter
this tie brings us to being one; which is why my love there'll never be the words I left her

OUR TEAMWORK,
WILL ALWAYS BE

what we are can't be broken
and that my princess, time after time I've spoken
and to seal the deal, all need be is our trust
but baby I've broken because my know, is the must
which means it's now my sexy your bodies craved
and within me, just for you such orgasms I've saved
therefore, my sexy, for only your beyond beautiful self I've gave you the shirt off my back, when
no one else was playing
which means my, I love you words are easy to believe; my sexy princess please comprehend what
I'm saying

and our teamwork will always last
promises between our connection, so solid has me always feel, lift off and blast
this branch of combination will surely keep us as one
and will cause us to always shine off any approaching scum
do you yet comprehend, it's now my sexy what our togetherness blossoms shiny colors
such beauty holds us in connection, and our special waters pave our path for the future

your sexy and special body romances my heart, which is why darling I'm in love
and other pours from your heart and mind; which is the fire of a beyond beautiful dove
and our unity causes us to keep a special lock, which is impossible to fade
check it, by our teamwork such has been made
our togetherness used our hearts and minds as one to shape our growth
many have tried but to touch our tie, can't even been seen by most
my love, one needs to understand, reason shiny characters untouchable beauty, for lifetime I'll
boast
therefore, sexy doll there's confusion, at just what I can do to grasp your attention and inform,
only you are wanted as my teammate
in meaning there won't be another choice
and by accepting the invitation, my hearts gratefulness
is always voiced
which stands as why, without any decorations I'm claiming you look good
my eyes never see any messy left overs, and are only caught by the ongoing rhythm of us, being
solid as wood

it's now baby our romance lives in a bonded togetherness
and with such is a meshed wall; which has me never feel less
my special love I will always claim. just you as my prize
it's now and will always never be left in any disguise
meaning baby, only your heart and mind's desired
therefore, I hunger to sexually work you to tired
you can't calculate the fire of my happy hormones
which when apart I always long for you to come home

here we are, and as we hold one another my heart smiles
and for you girl, my love runs for endless miles
therefore, do you yet comprehend I desire only, yes only you
meaning if the time ever comes, just my candy is who I choose

as time passes, I'm over taken by your engulfing beauty
which leaves me astonished and has me on knees
sweetie it's not possible to be understood, reason you're my girl how touched with overwhelming
joy I am
to have just you as my treasure is lifelong plan
therefore. my love just you has a home in my heart
the cuddly comfort you cause is reason there are no words to express my appreciation you gave
me the start

the days pass by but my gratitude we are the team tickles me crazy
these sudden jolts are why such happiness I have, you chose me
so, my beyond beautiful touch of love, upon myself dear angel cause the strong degree of glee
in meaning I just know for however long our love and unity will strengthen our tree
sexy sweetie it's now I only desire your jewel filled body
you must grasp on truth, dear angel the blessing, on can always lean
which is because I will always have overwhelming joy you and I are the team
that's because it's so beautiful it's no longer you and I but we
and our ravishing fire brushes aside all of life's weeds
I feel privileged you give myself the honor of within you planting my seeds
such is why I always desire your character and body
it's on those alone, for life I will feed
my gorgeous flower, it be just you I need
as my mate, there's no one else I desire to see
it's now my precious gift our joint work causes the blessed parade; which reveals our love's no
mystery

our furthering bridge ties our hearts together
there is such warmth in our to each other's hearts feathers
and it is within that bond we'll hold one another
and it is within this delicacy, for upcoming days our hearts will deliver definitely the most
satisfying flavor
which is why to give you my all will never be the chore
and that means reason you my flower have blossomed within I have chief and easily the
greatest score
that means my inspiration we have togetherness, which is our seal
and guarantees us the love strength deal
such a lock is held together through the bond of kisses and hugs
which is always the reason holding you is the must
yes, my sexy blessing when comes to all I just know you're the best
meaning when it comes to rating all, your gorgeous self is better than the rest
and baby there's no possible explanation to define because of our friendship the awesome
joyfulness that's sprouted and grown throughout me
which is why I know it was wise to establish you as my hearts key
such an infinite above all other blessing you are
at night, sexy candies thought of when I see any incredibly crafty star
that's reason teamwork's happiness prolongs in our step by step beat
our planted seeds, in time will blossom our furthering feet
then just how such magnificently superb beauty shines in your every step and all smiles; which
colors my spirit, heart and entire body

here we are and we've been at so many
our combo of duel, the surpassing tools carry us to being greater than all or any
my sexy spark as we come together infinitely so far beyond beautiful fruit of furthering begins
its activity
meaning my love within us is the bond which has been strengthened through our fruit filling
and impeccably done blossomed tree

I'm sure our partnership and love will always be
Which will carry us to pass by all of life's negativity
This develops our unique and precisely perfect beauty
Is it yet understood to describe you there's no possibility
Meaning the lifelong promise of unbearable love is to you
Which leaves myself with no other fragile flower to choose

What we have will always last
Which is reason like two who're wise didn't behave in the phase of fast
Even though the doors were open we took our time of dedication
And we'd ignored all obstacles which would cause destructive infection
Such had built or grown our bond to enhance in the flavor of lifelong friendship
That joy my love did and will always carry us to overcome every opposing and interfering ship
Such obstacles our teamwork will overcome
That victory guarantees us to in life with one another always dear have endless fun
Which is the lock of our hearts to one another and divinely colors our every step
And it's my promise to you I have kept
That my love will always brush aside all of life's blemishes
Ands my token to you which guarantees you can always trust my promises
Ands my truthful river of love, which flows from my spirit to embellish you with tickling kindness
That my sexy artwork is and will always be our timely fence
Which carries our bond to impress and be seen as one of a kind
This my adored and treasured art will always tickle with endless time
Meaning we'll be seen as ones to be like, such a loyalty like never been seen before
And our promising teamwork of coloring does and always will be graded as the highest quality score
As time passes our journeys color all newcomers
They are stunned at just why such a beauty like you is the one I can claim, I have her
Meaning there not be any words or possibility of description at just what you left or are from
And just why to me your heart and arms were open with, come, come, come
To that uprising does cause my heart to be embellished with lifelong furnaced fires of enhanced love
Such testimonial grounds of permanent beauty are encouraged by your promising heart; which is above
Meaning besides you, no one else has possibility of being better
I've not experimented but just know to your high grade there is no other
Therefore, there shall not be another angel who ever enters my life
With love like no other which has any ground anywhere in time
This my love lasts as why I have trusted truth in that our passage which embarks teamwork's bond
And colors us to an ever-living tunnel full of hugs and kissing fawn
An innocence of these grounds takes us beyond all the rest
Which heavily assists us in overcoming all the mess
That bouncing or pitter patter of grace broadens my horizon to what I see in our every step of friendship

My babe, it's in those knitted together locks of highs and dips
I understand in full, no matter what we can't be phased
Meaning when depression approaches, to lean on my shoulders will be present for all of days
Therefore, our love now excites new enchanting journeys of encouragement
We finally realize such beats we share carry our bond to new grounds of what's meant
Which is for you and I my dear to pass by all obstacles or any diversion
Diminishing or side wondering will always be defeated by our combination
Our security of bonded truth, means our love will always be enchanting
A whirlwind of love such is has my inner and outer being constantly smiling
A blessing you are, because morning, day and night you look good
Meaning when you wake up you fuel my hunger to feed on which I should
Meaning your food is easily better than the best
And can't be even nicked, by as one all the rest
Is it yet comprehended having you as my teammate, besides you has caused me to want nobody
Which be reason, as my one and only, you are for me

THERE MUST BE

Great amount of joy overcomes once you're present
This has me feel so definite
For sure I choose correctly
And knowing there's nobody better for me
Because you baby is my candy
Such passion leaves choosing you to be no mystery

Having you is why I'm in a maze of overflowed happiness
One of a kind is your filling joyfulness
Surely, it's you I'm expose to be with
It is clearly evident you girl are my finish
So now babe I must know, just where did you get the overwhelming kindness
Your character overtakes me, with a great bliss
I'm definitely not complaining but do not understand why you chose myself
Because to you, I see many flaws in self
In you babe I haven't found any
So now sweetie what's your secret, or let me in
Because sweetie I desire your finish

My dear sex machine our times of flavor have been naughty
Some would classify us as far above the highest degree
Then there are those who're interested but unable to make sense
I'm not mouthy but your characters beauties distance has no fence
This is when I'm overtaken by your endless flavors of so top of line delicious and definitely
pleasing fruits
Therefore, my sexy I'm over thrilled when it comes to my one and only, my body fits only one suit
Meaning sweetie there need not be any thought of another touching
Because to be each other's is our bodies only molding

You sex machine, up, down, and all around my emotions swirl
Just sight, then touch of you causes the orgasmic fire within me to unleash and like a wild storm
ongoingly twirl
So, so massively I hunger to fall deeper in love with you
My baby there are no words; in fact, it's impossible to define my appreciation it was the angel
I chose

— 109 —

I just don't comprehend your inner beauty which feeds fuel to that already blossomed flower in
your heart
And my delicate yet so tenderly precious love I just cannot explain my gratefulness you the
gorgeously pieced together art gave me a start
I'm privileged and greatly humbled just to claim you as the one who desires me
It's with you I just can't wait for our life's to ongoingly blossom seeds
True is the fact, there's literally nothing which can take me from your hands
Because dear sweetheart, our hearts are interwoven, which has given cheer to our sands
Therefore, my luscious candy the taste you give does nothing but please
Awesome blessing, to spend time with you brings me such ease

Description of you isn't possible
Such thanks and appreciation I have we're a couple
As the days pass by our bond strengthens
To always bring you comforting love and romance is my life long mission
I just do not understand why you have such inner beauty
It's as if pretty perfection blossomed all throughout your tree
Where's the end of your glamorous riches, because my love enjoys all your roads
And yes, it's evident within your peace, innocence has been sown
And my dear babe, it's true day by day I yearn your heart
There's no possible explanation which I can find to express this engulfed joy within; which is
reason you've given me a start

Your light brightens my heart
Which is why there's appreciation you gave me a start
And has me know to all others you can't be put on any chart
The taste of body teases, which tickles like a fancy sweet tart
So baby, I just cannot grasp onto where the blessing you are began existence
You're all around beauty to come from two I just can't find any sense
Which is why I yearn for who you are
And daily I long to be hugged and kissed by my star
And during sleep I dream of us locked as one
Which is why my sexy candy spending time with is so much fun
Having the privilege to hold in arms is the best gift of all
It's also why I know you'll never one who causes my mood to fall
Far past the best possible beyond beautiful blessing is the sexy candy that teases
And my emotions and heart, you my love are it for who pleases

Sexy love your fire has me craving your body
Being fueled by love our inferno fire has hold of me
It as simple as for you, from my heart the flames pour out
Reason I'm the one who protects from life's weeds, I am your scout
In our journeys we stray from the hiccups
We are destined to be together for life and such is because we have so much fun
It took some devoted expeditions but for you all I have is appreciation
And baby your in and out beauty doesn't surpass just some
From your heart and mind the perfection engulfs your body
Dear sweetie this explosive burst, is just not recognized by me
My dear peach the peace and love which flows from your every spoken word comforts my heart
Which is why I know my loyal devotion was so smart
And due to your characters positivity, my emotions are enchanted by your tart
With that scrumptious candy rockets of joy rush throughout me
Dear lullaby your every word is music to my heart
In our teamwork you definitely fulfill your part
Through that stronger and stronger we are fastened
Yes baby, as one we have grown and blossomed

The gift one is cannot be explained
When others approach, reason you're mine I'm not phased
Right as you're seen what floods isn't understood
Reason you accepted I don't have to claim I could or should
Before we came together, in me there was pollution
To grasp onto the gift you are, I just don't understand
To your heart, mind, and character I'm the devoted man

To comprehend in full what a peaceful touch of love, which you are can't be understood
Surely sweetie our bodies interlocking feels so good
You luscious baby, have me dumbfounded
The ripest love which pours from your heart verifies what I've founded
That means reason you're my girl heart belongs to you
My hearts your home and comprehend the blessing is mine; as being true
Meaning I desire to be the one you always use
And don't want any other
And long for us to unite, as blades on a feather
Day by day I taste all areas of your fragile body
And just know on me you can always lean

My love in such innocence you were pieced together
As my partner I never want another
There must be a reason my dear I earnestly hunger your legs, lips, character and body
It's in our rhythm of love causes day by day in, the innocent love I see
To grasp onto such priceless beauty, has me at a loss of words
To touch, then hold with aim of your body is always leaned towards
Once the magnificent beauty was seen, I reached the grade a score
Just having taste, will always cause the hunger for more and more
Not knowing when to stop, will always cause my fire to be active
The blessings we enjoy have reach of no limits
And that baby will always tickle my emotions
So thankful I am for me to enter I no longer need any type of permission
Just looking at you causes me to be speechless
Such a blessing, the joy which is within you has grounds of being limitless
And with this magnificent comfort my heart, spirit, mind and body are engulfed with
enchanting bliss
And that baby, is why not one moment, hand by hand I desire to miss
It is those emotions my love, that catapults me to an unbreakable bond
Is also reason besides you I do not want any other font
My dear sweetie, have you yet grasped onto just why love you are always class A plus
It's because what's key, from me to you is my whole hearted trust
Yes, your physical appearance, with no question pleases me but it's your beauty in every beat
that has hold of me
And you being the pretty princess you are is why you have and will always keep

I just cannot make sense to why you desire me
But to explain my appreciation, there's no possibility
I just cannot make sense to the grounds that I have; which has me to you any equality
Which has me honored when during troubles, on my shoulder you lean
And reason the friendship we live, it's you I feel and surely with joy my heart excites
My love, the fire lit emotions in my heart will always comfort due to fact you will always be
me light
And reason the friendship we live, our path will always be enjoyed
My dearest love it be you who shall always be my so, so hungered toy
It's true babe my seed and your soil will blossom from you, the beyond beautiful tree
Meaning my yummy and precious candy, do you yet comprehend, as my one and only I will
only desire your body

It's true babe my eyes are stuck on only you, and this is because my spirit and heart have been hardwired to just have attraction for you alone
Which is why you can confidently know, it's in my heart you will always home

Where my love are you from, I just don't comprehend your in and out beauty
I can't make sense on hoe you began life within any she
There is no understanding, on how you are from two
Which is because the preciousness your heart, mind and spirit have, isn't understood how it has source as being you
And that my love is why I desire no one else
Ands why I've placed you on the highest shelf
It's also reason I only crave your lips, breasts and entire body
I want no other to touch my taste buds and to be that which I see
You are my one and only, which I desire
My babe it's not possible for there to be another which is higher

Sweet and sexy you are
You darling, are my guiding star
And it's just you, day by day I yearn and hunger
You are it, meaning screw all other colors
As my one and only you are it
And to touch, to hold, there are no limits
Such the lucky man I am
My dear sweet and sexy babe I'm your number one fan
My sweet pearl you have a specially crafted home in my heart
And baby your all-around beauty is so, so profoundly stellar it cannot be put on any chart
I just do not understand how the priceless pearl like you exists
But the key point, you, you beyond beautiful diamond chose me; which has me have the endless win

Besides you I do not want another
As I wake up to at night taking rest knowing you're my friend has me satisfied I can state, I chose her
And during these times such past and present tense fiery jolts of passionate love engulfs me
So baby, it's within you my heart beats
And in mine the uplifting joy you cause brings such ticklish glee
Which is reason, for you day by day my heart sings
I cannot find the possible reason your gorgeous self-desires no other but me

Which is why it's just you I adore, love, touch and see
Your taste has such a flavor that for you causes myself to hunger and feed
Ands reason there's just one unlocking possibility and only my beyond beautiful angels' heart
is the key

It's just you, I desire to enter
There are many others who're willing, but for them I don't even bother
Then there's blossoming flowers, which within my heart and spirit, with flavor filling fruits so
delightfully and rhythmically color
My baby so mesmerized by you I get lifted to a mysterious mirage, and being filled with love,
within my heart creates a variety of multicolor
So fortunate I am, that your warmth comforts like the mid of summer
And for that my sexy candy is why I'm grateful you are my cover
But still my flavored delight it's just you who I long to embrace
So scrumptious and sexy delight, from me it's just you who'll never be erased
It's that alone, which will always comfort
And is why, the taste of you will never be tart
So baby, I'm still dumbfounded on just where your beauty's from
And girl, I'm just not talking about what's visible but's what's within heart and mind and our
special times which enchant with awesome fun

I do not comprehend, just where the beautiful gift you are is from
To taste and hold you, I always so intensely crave some
It's you baby, I can't find the words to express how thankful I am
For you girl, I'm always your number one fan
Pearls of beauty stream from every breath
On that, I do day I so, so cherish our every step
Love of my life, there are just no words which describe my fire for you
Which is why I'm spoiled, because it's I you choose
Yes, it could be put in past tense, but through the stress day after day, for your one and only it's me
Which is reason, for each other's our ongoing devotion are the keys
So priceless love I just wish there was a possible definition which would even have the slightest
touch of describing the complete package you are
But it's not possible for there to be, therefore it's now and always will be you diamond are my
guiding star
Meaning in those down times, just a thought of you my tasty candy arouses my emotions
And it's on your body I look forward to rubbing and caressing within those lotions

So my sexy, just what is the reason the priceless beauty like you exists
As life passes by I'm well aware of the beauty you live but how
Such a sweet and special treat your body is
And your hearts roses of love, I never want to miss
I just do not comprehend where a beautiful blessing like you is from
Which is why for you I will always come

When we kiss the peace, which engulfs isn't understood
Reason your in and out beauty I disregard any thought about if or should
But my dear there's just no possible way a definition for why exists
To describe your awesomeness there's just no capability to find you on any list
Your character brightens me like the night is by the stars
Still, you lovable sexy I'm stuck on just trying to define how marvelous you are
And day by day I'm startled by your outpouring cheer
My love, it's you I crave and always hunger my so, so special dear
Therefore, do you yet comprehend your life's causing ongoing glee
Which is why for you I'm humbled to on my knees
My dear honey I'm dumbfound for why, but appreciative that you desire me
And baby I so look forward to building our tree
From it girl, our soil will blossom more and more beyond beautiful fruit
Which is why baby, it is you I will always choose
There's confident surety, it's you I never want to lose
And about such I will always keep that
So delicious candy, you always being supremely awesome is a true fact

You are and always will be my one and only, and within you it's my goal to install my seeds
And it's on my shoulder you can always lean
Meaning my dear so sexy in my arms, you are
It's foolish to rate your wonderfulness on any chart
I've dreamt of beyond beautiful angels, but your gorgeousness puts all of them to shame
In and out your specialness will never leave me the same
I do not know where it exists, but there just has to be reason for a beauty like you taking breath
Dear love the peace within is above all
And reason my appreciation, causes me to proudly stand tall
But still pretty flower showers of beauty, from your heart engulf me
That so gentle lullaby, to my heart's the key
And that my beyond beautiful fire continuously brings me ease
Because so special blessing there are no words, which define how fantastically you please

Your every breath lets loose rivers of love
Which causes me, to all definitely feel above
Such fragile innocence your heart and mind live out, always causes me to comfortably rest
That sexy blessing has me never feel less than the best

As I sit and ponder or try to determine there is no sense to just fathom where the avenue such
joyfulness within began
Better than you, there's not any other woman
So grateful I am, for where your infinite glee rooted
When you were first seen, in astonishment I was muted
Meaning my luscious babe, it's deep within your core I yearn to soak within your body
It's this craving, on a daily basis gets longed by me
Do you yet grasp onto the concept, within my heart you are my seed
And on that day, our overflowing happiness does satisfy all
Which is reason, within my mind I have the rowdy ball
So luscious candy, for your hungered taste there's no possibility to define
And to enjoy the delicacy you are, it's on that token I will always be first in line to dine
Oh girl, it's you love who in me has that life-long home
So infinitely fabulous you are, it's literally impossible to clone
Just absorbing the touch rockets myself to unknown lands
I so look forward to rubbing my hands through your hair, like the wind tickles the sand
In our relationship I do recognize you are not phony
For that my babe is why, as I breathe only you will have the key

Seeing you clearly is what I attempt to do
Because of such, it's just you I choose
Not wanting any other
When it comes to the rest, I don't even bother
The journey filled walk we've shared brings me entire fulfillment
Because my sexy rose, I know for me you are meant
It's clearly evident that besides there's not any desire to embrace, kiss, spank or sleep with
another
My so, so special and sweet tasteful delicacy, there's massive appreciation you are my lover
There's no height my giddiness maxes at
Fulfilled to the max, as the matter of fact
The joyfulness which blossoms throughout just cannot be controlled
You are my teacher and I look forward to being schooled

My inner fire's fueled by your bedtime lessons
So scrumptious you are, your body is my delicatessen
And that my dear, verifies how you are so uncontrollably sexy
Which is why, literally only desire your body

OUR TRUST'S UNBREAKABLE

In our day-by-day relationship, such uplifting enjoyment your presence causes
These journeys of thrill and positivity, in awe roots upon me such a pause
In our rhythmic love, between us melodies of sexual contact blossoms
And it's that fuel which ignites our flames of inferno passion
Now I just know, my lovely peach not better but even close to equal doesn't exist
The building began when our bond refused to exit
The belief in each other's steps flourishes naughty fruit
Such always delivers our untouchable root

The lock holding our hearts together is sinched with a joint love
Us following each other causes no other to be above
In such rhythm delicacy enchants our inner beings
And to one another, with colorful romance our spirit's sing
The keys which secure our lock has foundation of trust
Me within you, and your body on mine is surely the must
For us both, there is no type of doubt in each other
It's true our reliability in each, has one of a kind color
Meaning babe, I feed off the teamwork and thirst for your sport
Because sexy sweetie, it is in you my trust has reached the sweetest score
Meaning darling, from within, for you my trust pours
You know it babe, you are it for who I love
For your every breath and beat, I can never get enough
So, my honey sickle, of you there can never be enough taste
Which is key reason, as the only like is you for all days
These feelings, which rooted from our trust is surely no phase
Within me, reason my gears for, my mind and heart's set a blaze
It's now girl, I long to enjoy more and more what we've built
It's now girl, you must know when I'm in need, you comfort as my quilt
Our security is held together by the foundation
And such a birth rooted within the day-by-day pension
You see having trust in each other is the food to our riches
Not by financial state, but greater than such feeds the bountiful promise
That which we have built
These grounds cause when needing a shoulder to rest, on partner we tilt

For and on one another we rely
Such beauty mystifies, and just embellishes I
So beautiful is our within each, mold
It's true, when the times of depression approach, my love now and will always protect you
from the cold
And when disturbance approaches, having you love causes me to remain calm
When needing warmth, your skin is my balm
The fire our reliance has built, is the lock and key
And in our tie, blessings fuel our tree
Fulfillment of each carries us as we achieve the fruitful missions
It's that my dear which feeds my hunger to cause satisfaction
Dear, dear love because our bond is so solid, for another there's not any notion
And sexy your soft skin is the hepatizing potion
Such rambunctious flavor is the delicious taste one feeds
Which is why, day in and out its our lock I need

Here we are, and being one day by day we build
It is in these passionate romances, as the team we grow our skills
True it is on the day-by-day basis, for each other's assistance we rely
Through the dependance our connection reaches past the sky
The growth doesn't stop, because there being an end doesn't exist
My sweet and sexy, so, so gorgeous love my trust in can't be measured on any list
And yours in me is evidently clear
It shines in one's unbreakable gears
Meaning our trustworthy loyalty is a gleam filling light within our everlasting stronghold
Such blaze we live will carry on our family trees connection; which from day one I was sold
In other words, being so strong our fire with ease our fire will burn through all those
significant times
This my precious does and will always shine light the trust built; which is definitely so precious
and fine
Not caring what others think in my opinion, dainty and precisely fine is your perfect body
And it's the glamorous touch which always pleases me
It is the promising gift alone, that our trust delivers which furthers our relationship
In meaning the coloring that the built coloring, feeds the interlocking lips
This fasten is held together by the unchanging trust our held together and strong friendship
Such firmness delivers such a glistening blaze of light
This feed blossoms the honey sickle of a genuine bond to our sight
So, great's the furthering victory the limitless love our trust victors with

And that alone my dear love is why we'll always have the loud and proud win
It is the cheer and glee for one another, which outlasts any challenge
My sweet love, without you I never want to finish
My luscious, so soothing is ones sweet, sweet skin
That favorable taste has me ongoingly know I have the win
Such a promising token you definitely are
Meaning my trusts assured confidence has me know you're never far

Our bond brings our trust more and more strength
For you, my dear sweet love my emotions have a limitless length
And within our tie berries so, so color your heart with glorious love
Which is why there's no existence to trusting another above

Watching you causes joy within to flicker
It is always claimed by myself, there's massive gratitude I can confidently say, I have her
In such teamwork we live, ongoing is the always lasting trust
From me to you, just to taste that score is always a must
Do you yet understand, you can always rely on me
For it's that treasure alone, which furthers our seed
So baby, it's now time we realize our connection will never be broken
Held together, by our love knitted trust is why are the shoe in for more than enough
It you my pearl, I so long to caress not and feel
Which is why, for you babe I'm afraid to kneel

It's with you, and just is who has my mind, spirit, heart and all existing fire
Which is why there's no question on will ever, because I know of you, I will never grow tired
Such a bond is harnessed by our untouchable trust
Which is beaming for all to see, and causes those to jealously yearn and strive with the belief,
that is our must
The gleaming brightness our togetherness shines awakens the sleepy and forwards the lost
Which is because our pieced together art of the friendship, and that alone my love shall and will
keep us; without any type of cost
Then my sweet and precious flower, it is on your cheeks I desire my lips to be it for what as
one kisses
Which stands as the core reason, I just know myself is not ever the one who misses
And that's reason just you are it for who I love

Which stands as the evidence I just know, it is within your feel, inner and outer beauty the fragile innocence lived and within shines the softness and beyond beauty of the most pieced together dove
Such innocence reveals itself in every step and breath you live
Which is core reason, for you just to please, over and over I will always give
That is my definite promise from my heart to yours, and will always be the key reason my spirit and heart has been knitted for only you
Which lives as my reason, there just is no possibility for there to be any other sex for me to choose
I have the all-time victory; yes, girl just because you desire me alone
Which reveals itself as being the one and only choice for the best is, just you alone

It's our trust between and for each that feeds my heart
Therefore, morning, day, evening and night it's within me, for one another; within our teamwork draw out is a chart
And as we grow closer the bond, we share builds stronger in such a glorious fire
Therefore, in such a bridge our trusts building strength grows stronger and higher
For it is evident we shall build to such a height that is ongoing
Therefore, our trust in each will always keep the blessing over and over coming
And it's all because whole heartedly, for one another there's whole hearted trust
Therefore, it is just your body, heart, mind and spirit which is my entire must

Thanks to, https://images.unsplash.com/photo-1517488948216-e473cee81e23?ixid=MnwxMjA3fDB8M
HxwaG90by1wYWdlfHx8fGVufDB8fHx8&ixlib=rb-1.2.1&auto=format&fit=crop&w=465&q=80

3 B'S

Better than you isn't possible
Bringing me constant relief is you, the one who has no troubles
When thoughts of you arise, being full of joy I always catch myself singing
Which is because you and you alone are my beyond beautiful blessing
Such a inner and outer beauty cannot be matched
That's right my perfect love, the all-around adorable package you are cannot be touched
So, so sexually precious is your fragile and tenderly pieced together body
And that dear love, has stolen me
Yes, my gorgeous piece of rare art, you are one of a kind
Sexy love, the words don't possibly exist to express the gratitude you are mine
The passion of my fire, has such eruption the rhythm of our beat, soothes as we sleep
Our tie will never fade, which would cause in need to leap
It is within our love the beyond beautiful heart, which belongs draws me in closer
Reason you give me the honor of claiming you as my brilliant blessing, and hottie I proudly
state myself has her

i have victory, because you want to be my woman
i will always smile, because it's my angel who's seen
i can't get enough, which means for you I'll always come
i am always hungering your body, which means for that feel myself is the biggest feen
i don't get enough taste of you
i cannot find possibility, for that to be
i currently and always will know, by I yearn to be in use
i have prearranged, for to be the tree

I've memorized the pitter patter between every heartbeat
Which is why on equal ground we seat
Yes, sweet and gorgeous love of life there's no possible existence to be better than you
And that is my fire lit drive to literally always be at your use
So, my perfect and superb sex machine, it's just you who's lit my heart on fire
Which provides harvested greens of fragrant fruits and naughty delicacies
These untamed flavors pour from our lips and colors one another spirit
Such tasteful fruit is the ongoing forwarding our heart and mind seeks
Our bond's so strong, for one another we will never leak
Meaning sweet, sweet and always close by love, there is no chance for there being anything greater

My sexy, such beauty yourself withholds only strengthens
For it has no possible chance to lessen
I only desire you, and just long to taste what's within and always the beyond beautiful body
As better than the best, just you are the sum
It's clear I don't want any other body, and your inner self is that blessing

We hold onto one another, that causes me to not desire any other
We have become one, which has a rare and genuine color
We have a bond that cannot be separated
We have such a strong love; it just provides no possibility to be faded
We embark on one after another mission
We have built upon, so we are the others ignition
We fuel our fire to keep on
We warmth the others heart, as for the partner each is the sun
We cuddle in the other's arms
We have blessed to the partner, in being the uplifting charm
We live such a victory, in the embraced one on one time
We will always be satisfied, because no longer do we need to find

As we ponder about what's desired each other should be
It is in such romance there outlasts tickles of delightful candy
There's only one conclusion, being satisfied just by one another
And it's within our love's enjoyment we'll continue the making of sister and brother
In such a flavored journey of ongoing
Is a continuous fulfilling feeding
Of such a specialized token of love
Which is why besides you no other will ever be above
Meaning, you being love of my life have just one home in me
And it's within where your presence makes sure there's no weeds
In this area's where you'll always have a home
Within our relationship, as us being one we hone

Our hearts have been sown as one
Our times of pleasure, to and for the other we have so much fun
Our times of thrilling fire causes us joyfulness
Our combination has myself just know you're meant
Our love's pieced together by such romance of inspired times of glee
Our timed together friendship, in bricks of love is held together

Our times of fulfilling satisfaction, maintain immense flavor filling fruit
Our times of relationship is why, by you I don't mind being abused
Our knotted together instinct plays as the core reason for why within the lasting teamwork such friendliness keeps us as one
Our hearts molding, within the sanctioned love that's shared a blessed covering of cuddled embrace, assists us in the shared and embroidered connection
Our shared tie shall outlast all journeys; big and small
Our love's unbearable fire burns to nothing all side wandering distractions
Our texture of comforting ointment blesses us and sums up the soothing embrace

So, my dear lovable package it's now and always will be together we hold such a fire together
It always will be, sexy lady there's indulgent on tasting your tasting your body
Because the body before is the enjoyment, as it's tasted there's a promising richness of overflowing inner hormones
Baby, my sweet and sexy kiss of love so perfect it's impossible to clone
Not even anywhere close
And there's endless appreciation my beyond beautiful blessing, even though there are others you have chosen I
This has no possible reason for why such is, and outlasts any time relationship does cause but concludes with one heart
In meaning the love we carry for one another's always pushing the greens of the richness we withhold
On day-by-day basis, I love you, we can proudly claim we told

You're with me, and for that I'll always be on cloud nine
You're unable to be matched, and that's easy to know
You're better than all the rest, and for this I'm literally speechless
You're the one I know who's meant for me which outlast any other existing fact
You're one of a kind, and so especially unique I don't understand how you exist
You're such a priceless blessing no matter what I'll always have thanks
You're a belt of blessings, which will never ending be enjoyed
You're promising richened food, on daily basis I hunger to taste
You're a in and out beyond beautiful character ongoingly brightens my heart, and it's that alone which furthers me in my step by step
You're the infinite blessed character, which colors me with wildly tasteful and so delicious delicacies
You're better than the best possible, and at any time I'll gladly admit that

You're by far the best possible in bed, which is known by the up to sky orgasms I always enjoy
You're one who has unbearable beauty
You're a beauty with a heart of endless riches
During our times of emotional fulfillment, I enjoy massive moments of love
It's in these times of favorable passion firesome jolts from our hearts connect
My dear babe, it's now and always our times of favorable gears will guide us in each journey we take part in
In meaning sweetie, your beyond beautiful, so blessed self, next to will always keep me in the beside seat
I just cannot lose sight of you
For lovable spark, it's with you alone my heart has inferno fire to be with
And without you I never want to be
In meaning the tickling of pieced together teamwork we shine
And it's within our building the taste we deliver to each is so, so fine
Just to feel, kiss and lick you brings our enjoyment closer together
Within the love we've built there are no periods
Reason because our ever-living love shall outlast all battles
Which is because the teamwork we've built carries our times of our journeys within such colors of ongoing happiness

Us is the connection that'll always be
Us, and not desiring any other is reason just you I choose
Us is the friendly teamwork, that'll not never fade
Us, we are the conjoined and unbreakable package
Us is our forming and will always be the joined love
Us which means our beyond beautiful teamwork will always shine above
Us, for one another's enjoyment such the blessing we are
Us, as one we've come so far
Us, our direction is only forward
Us is what we began as and as the team we will always be
Us has our primal answer, for we're not greater than another
Us has gears of being one
Us, through all struggling hardness our times of conjoined tie does and will always overcome any feud
Us, for each other we're the food
Us and in such we color with overpowering shades of trickled passion
Us is what you and I are and will always be

As time passes by times of glee we enjoy,
Which is reason we are one another's toy,
Is it yet understood by you I cannot enjoy anyone better,
The most effort can be put forth, but it's not possible to exist,
Desiring anyone else will never be,
For it is within the jolts of rippling fury, which coat our heart with tenderized flowers,
And it is upon such times of blessing your beyond beauty shines,

Together, we pass by any questionable times
Together is how we overcome all struggles
Together be the only fashion we must take part in
Together we carry one another throughout all tasks and adventures
Together is our unbearable teamwork
Together will always be our united connection
Together is and will always be my intention
Together, and times revealed cannot be damaged
Together is our combined friendship
Together highlights the continuous fun we have
Together is where we stand and will always live

In a flavored ride of sweet passion, it's with you I desire to hold
For it is my beyond beautiful blessing, myself is within your mold
There you lay and it's upon your cheeks the innocence about lives out
Just for your touch I've been driven
Not desiring to feel of any other or the kiss of another
You and you alone are my sexual passion
Not wanting any other feeds my fire
Such a harmony plays in your pitter patter breath
There is no understanding on how such a beyond beautiful blessing such as yourself even exists
There must be a reason for why such kindness takes breath
It just cannot be reason, because it's you
If that were such, there'd be many more
Which has myself know, reason you've chosen me, my love at the top of the list I've scored
True it is my eyes just see one beyond beautiful blessing
Reason that's all there is capable to
Which is because that's all that exists
And there have been others, but to that mess I just shove
Therefore, it's just you who is my one and only love

My timeless heart, is because you live within
There's no possibility for there to be an end to my boundless love for you
Which is why I desire to always be used
There always will be unending friendship with you
It's true during those orgasmic moments I live to always feel your touch
Cannot enjoy enough, meaning love of life I hunger that inner and outer body so, so superbly much
Meaning my dear love, it's with just you I desire to embrace, then hold
I'm well aware, as my only you have been told
Now it's my mission to day-by-day shine such a mold
For it is my mission to continuously color your heart with comfort
Life cannot continue if I do not cause upon you oncoming gifts
Sweet, sweet and especially adorable love, as my beyond beautiful blessing you have already filled me with that needed lift
In our romantic flavors, blossoms uplifting genuinely
Which has strongly fastened our unbreakable honesty

Thanks to, https://images.unsplash.com/photo-1585578911801-e4f8582859a8?ixid=MnwxMjA3fDB8M HxwaG90by1wYWdlfHx8fGVufDB8fHx8&ixlib=rb-1.2.1&auto=format&fit=crop&w=462&q=80

My love is always yours
My commitment you can always rely on
My heart, just know always belongs to just you
My dance always is at step your hearts every beat
My breaths occur with just you on mind
My steps continue because you're my fire to live
My heart beats with just you in it
My uncontrollable passion to press on is feed by my living glee for you
My tickles and romances are for you to enjoy
My oncoming times of enrichened blossoms are reason you're my one and only
My harmonical beat for you is coated with your love
My feelings for cause me too never have enough
My and your love sums up the complete package

It's for our times of thrilled ongoing passion, we outlast any hiccup
Within these times continuing on is our flavors of sexual blessings
So, my sweet love ongoing is the partnership we have
While we make love it's our tasty body we enjoy
And it is in these moments of enjoyment our lips enjoy new tastes
In meaning my love, it's during such enjoyment I will always cause you enjoyment
And such carefulness I'll be sure to coat you with
Just know my love there's not one more I desire to touch
It's easily known there's no other life being, who can be loved as much
The cradled love I have for you meets no boundaries
In meaning you can always be confident there's a man who loves you more than what's most
possible
Such gears only fueled by your tasty body
The genuine lock happens to be our togetherness
We have built the team, and such was with the assistance of my beyond beautiful blessing

You are one of a kind
You have me sold
You are not able to be topped
You genuinely are my loyal partner
You aren't able to be imaged
You are the gift I'm determined to never lose
You have never been heard of
You are in the class, which cannot be touched

You are with, in my one heart
You will never leave every thought I have
You cannot comprehend the depth of my whole hearted sincere love
You are honest with me and I'm genially loyal to you
You and you alone have a home in my heart
You are within my every uplifting thought; which are many
You are the one and only woman who has love; which belongs to
You have been carved within the core of my heart
You have given and are it for who with
You baby are it, for who's on mind, as I take every breath
You sweetie assist me in dissecting the mess
You make this possible by, you're in and out blessed beyond beautiful presence
You stun and amaze me
You and I provide such blessings
You with myself have developed life-long happiness
You, yes you my sexy bombshell are it for who I adore and love

Better than the best, you easily are
There's appreciation I have the golden star
Time with has shows me, I have the cream of the crop
Therefore, I always am on top
The beauty withheld, just cannot be fathomed
To comprehend the blessing one is, it's not possible to be determined
To grasp onto the beyond entire package the sexy pearl is cannot be done
Bountiful I am reason your beauties so much fun

Dear love, it's not possible for me to understand how I'm worthy of a kiss
But myself does know to go without never wants to be missed
And it's with, the love built grows stronger
Also reason there's thanks myself can state, I have her
It's love for, that fills the heart
And's reason my feelings for cannot be on any chart

I AM ON FIRE FOR YOU

My heart has a scorching fire within
And making it better, we've produced beautiful kin
Reviewing what you are, myself can't think of a change to improve
For you babe, mountain after mountain I would move
To all those lame reasons that come to head about why I shouldn't give you more than my all;
screw those excuses
Just how exceeding all, can be done confuses
But sweetie it's simple my heart, mind, spirit, every breath, and all upcoming have your name
etched in and hungry for you to use
Which is why it's my life's mission to only have you, as the one I choose

My body is always ready for you to use
And is for no one else to choose
Dear love, is it yet realized just you have a home in my heart
Just you and you alone, is it for who I've given the start
Your fire ignites, fulfills with warmth and tickles all my heart; with enchanted peace
It is only you, for myself will entirely please
Besides you, I just do not want any other
Which is because, equal or better than it's impossible for there to be another
Meaning my darling, I have endless appreciation you chose me as your one and only
And there's appreciation, day by day on your body I can feed
The fire running throughout I, builds stronger as time passes
Enough of you can never be reached or possibility that anyone surpasses
Sexy sweetie is it for the fireball my lips desire
And of your inferno one never tires
Of the beyond beautiful blessing you are, it's guaranteed I'll never fade away
In meaning, I will always be on your side; for all of days
Reason for such outlasts pieced together secured feathers
The full of flavor bond is held together by our enriched and passionate tethers
Just to feel, then to rub, moisturize and kiss betters me in all ways
Having you lye next to me, gives me fuel for the upcoming day
And as we interlock such beauty our togetherness blossoms great romance between
The most thankful does not define myself; you are in my team
There aren't feelings for any other sex; by which means I don't want any other
Meaning sweetie my lips don't desire the taste of another

The body I have longs for your touch and hungers your warmth
The enjoyment you cause only adjusts my penis north
So, so beautiful and sexy love it's not possible for me to desire anyone else
Which is because as the winner you're at the top of my shelf

Only you are it, for who I desire
Of you babe I will never grow tired
For me to hold, caress, romance and love you is the best possible gift
Yes, babe you give me that needed lift
Within your heart are ongoing treasures
There is appreciation it can be claimed, I have her
In & out myself is made for just you
Besides the rose, there's no one else to choose
The heart belonging to beats nothing except love
Our relationship causes the ignited fire to have me feel above
Beyond beautiful are the smiles which portray your innocence
I mean sexy sweetie to have the rose as my one and only, only makes sense
To wrap my arms around you and embrace the fire you cause betters me, in all ways, and the
positive boost doesn't leave me the same
This joyfulness is so rowdy it's not easy to contain
In the uplifting thrill you shake, rattle, roll and tease me with pieces together such a harmony of
love and gears for ongoing bliss
Till this day and it will always last, not being able to see my rose I never want to miss

The best existing sexy charm, yourself is entirely satisfying to my heart, mind, pleasurable
areas and sprit
My constant desire for your body, literally has limit
Which is to the widest width and highest peak
Us just hanging out and conversing; I am the biggest feen
For each other, our constant teamwork is addictive
Together as the loyal partnership, we will always live
And you my so delicious lollipop, it's you who day by day I desire to lick
And baby, just knowing you and I are in love satisfies me
And is reason I name you my hearts key
Meaning my sex machine, you are it for who I crave
When depression approaches, reason you I feel saved
Better than you, just doesn't exist
From what we have, my dear love I'll never desire an exit

Because my sexy pie, it's you and you alone who has my eyes
And baby, for our life's I'll give it my all at making sure it's in no disguise
Meaning my special love the urge for more's been lit by your glee and of you, will always have me need
This has sum to the core fact, for me there's no other better than you
And is the only reason, just you I will always choose

Just to feel causes sparks to soar, and my inner stars shine bright
For it's you alone my dear darling I can't get enough of, and will always beam the mighty light
There is no fulfilling my hunger for you
And sweet, sweet sexy candy, to my lips your satisfying taste is always new
So blissful is your every breath, which always has me right on top
I'm so comforted by the tickling romance of one's body, and there's confidence from such relaxation I will never drop
It's that sexy moisture, the so luscious candy one is, which unleashes my hormones on a crazy rampage
Whenever tasted you light me, being your body is the sage
Whenever needing the comfort of a beyond beautiful dove
To feel and hold can only be done by my love

It is you my sexy light, who ignites that soothing fire
And it be true, of you I will never tire
There it is, the harp of innocence which colors your hair
If there's ever any struggles just remember my love it's you who is my never-ending fair
Meaning there might be times of worry or fear, but in the end, I'll always embrace fun
For these gears always cause me to shift to just that my sexy bun\
It's also reason myself is first in line as the number one fan
Baby, the fire lighting sex machine who I need more of
In meaning it's the fire lighting one get enough
Also, there's sum of being the torch is always yearning
Such the excitement you are, you never leave me yawing
So touched is one, which is reason the tasty and blissful enjoyment deliciousness the blessing feeds
Such causes production of not weeds, but only greens

What a delicacy the delicious food one is
Such a satisfying fulfilling delivers your finishing bliss
Ending because, even at times of sexual pleasure to fulfill comes that orgasm power
This firesome jolt causes me to feel high like an unbreakable tower

That is where our treasure lives, for inside the conjoining bond we share
This unity keeps us together as the team
And's my guarantee on me you can always lean
Because sweet, special, satisfying and sexy baby so, so blessed does one feel to have you as my
woman
So happy I am, you are definitely the finish and always the one and only sum

So uniquely beautiful, in my eyes
This treasure sends me to the sky
It's like I'm on an unknown high
Such fragrant powder one is why I'll never say or live, goodbye
The fire within me causes the urge within to blossom unknown flavors
It is on that alone I desire to always savor
For the beautiful aroma you let off, entirely pleases me in all ways
And comes as the primal reason, for you my heart will be on fire for all days

The passion for, just cannot be understood
It's known at those times of sexual curiosity, to always lean on should
Such orgasmic excitement blossoms with my pearl being felt
For it's in the fire enticing angels hold I just melt

The hunger for more intensifies my emotions
Our fire builds in the step-by-step motion
It's on your body fancy gears blossom flavorful colors
Love's fire lit taste causes me to not desire another
Which causes the tasteful rainbow of enjoyment
Dear blessing, such is why only with one another is meant
Babe I cannot grasp onto the all-around beauty which brightly shines
Blessed I am, because on body myself dines
So precise is the graphing the peace filled heart belonging to required
Such the greatly fabulous art one is, from myself will never get tired
Meaning dear lovable peach, nothing can compete with you
Which is why I know wisdom's intact with who to choose
This inferno within isn't easy to contain
And as time passes, meaning as our connection grows closer the flames of passion never leave
me the same
Yes hunny bun, my sugar on top this flavored parade of excitement leaves self as your number
one fan

Therefore, in a dumfounded state I am
While time passes by, the connection-built blossoms more and more
Which causes one to know mine is the highest possible score
And that's reason, my flame rooting blessing, day by day of one's body there's desire to dive
deep and explore
There's fun and enjoyment, whenever hungry it's the blessed beyond beautiful angel's body I get
to tour
Such the honor it is, just to have the privilege to touch
That love's desired so, so much
It's with and you alone my heart longs to feel and massage
The oncoming passionate flowers, from flood like a beyond beautiful collage
These trickles of sparks are naughty but soothe my mind with nasty thoughts
Sexy baby, there's great appreciation you were caught
Couldn't ask for anyone better
That's why there's always thanks I can state, I have her

No other woman is better than
No other is a more lovable friend
With will always be
With just you, is all I can see
Having as mine is my one and only desire
Having just you is why I'll never grow tired
Because of, on the top I'll always be
Because we provide the ripest fruits, our love is the ripest tree

TOGETHER WE PROVIDE FORWARDING

For what we've made our life's deliver mystical fruits and enchant with soothing oils
Then sweetheart it's the interlocking of our lips which seal the freshest and most superb soil
In that my dear babe is where you'll find the seal to our hearts key
Because you're my partner I've won; with absolute guarantee
It's clear, for our tasteful love there is no finish line
Such happiness blossoms, because my body is yours and you mine
A true guarantee of top of the line you, my special love easily are
Sexy blessing from an unknown land your in and out peaceful beauty is greater than the
brightest star
True it be, as time passes by one's heart continuously beats fireworks of love
And it's true through our kind gestures to each we always keep one another feeling above
Such passion must and does have the permanent marking
Hidden blessing it may seem, but for my dear love keep mind open therefore there'll never be
any finding

Here is where we last
Not taking our steps slow or fast
In this gracious pattern, in secured teamwork we overcome any barrier
Because togetherness is held onto makes the situation merrier
Which means all difficulties are outlasted
Such trust given and received brings us together, in holding closer and closer; as the bond's
fastened
And it happens like the wind carries leaves
Love's sinched as one from you to me
Not being finished, together our infinite friendship outlasts all the sidewinding darkness
Which is reason, from heart to heart and spirit singing to other is endless bliss
Meaning my love, better than you isn't possible
Even every breath is its own individual
To comprehend even the slightest bit the beyond beautiful gift shines colors which aren't known
by any
Attempts to grasp the concept has been attempted by many
Crazy in love with and liking the fashion you live
Making it better, on a daily basis to one another daily we always give
Which blossoms the fuel that feeds and drive, so as one we are
Baby, it's simple for me to know, sexy blessing is my star
And with my fire lit heart, burning for you

Thanks to, https://unsplash.com/s/photos/heart-on-fire

My emotions soar high; to an indescribable height
This passion has me on an addictive high
The love for, even by me cannot be understood
And causes thanks, that our love's more solid than purple heart wood
So sexually special sweetheart, it is you babe who leaves hungering more
The naughty taste of those ripe lips leaves me knowing I have the primal score
Meaning girl, besides no other will ever soothe my passions
Which is reason our special times deliver adored sessions
Within our rowdy times the shared laughs build the chemistry to being more solid
The uplifting journeys we live, as growth is closer, we'll deliver more kids
Such passion continues on this roller coaster of orgasmic joy
Sweet and especially sexy dear, I'm so full of glee the rights belong to be known as, beyond beautiful blessing's toy
These happy times overflow my heart and spirit with fulfilled sensational flourishing
And sexually special babe, of course I'll never regret my hearts promising
The ongoing emotions shared color our hearts with the firmer security
Reaching this goal, reason the forwarding friendship assists the continuous happiness

Blessed togetherness embraced and built provides our best, and nothing less
Seriously sweetie, having anyone else I never want that day to exist
Which is why as my sexual partner, just you are on my list
To be precise, dear love of life nothings better than holding than caressing and I indulge your hugs which are covered by the favored kisses
That's reason I'll never be one living as on such the one who misses

Within our candies such delight tickles in the forwarding urge for more
These delicious delicacies enjoyed, as for one another are that just right core
So dear blessing like no other being the team player with has myself always know I have the victory
The win we live causes I to always feel like the main shot of the party
Building journeys are a furnace to the continuous steps done together
Therefore, about those side baring problems I don't even bother
Love, it's not possible for there to be any better than and such has me feel like I have a win

While we lie next to one another, mine & your every heartbeat is in sync
And the hottie you are, tied in with my emotions carries our connection to having the conjoining link
Our lights feed by the love we live
For one another, on a daily basis our friendship gives
As two hands lock together, it's used as a tool
In meaning, just seeing the joy we shine is used to school
And my dear love the beautiful blessing we are is coated with innocent harmony
That alone sexy sweetie, is used to feed
In such blessed enjoyment our teamwork blesses those who know not of
And it is that seed alone, which shines our love

Our steps of relationship love shape the upcoming days
For my sexy toy, to bring myself comfort thoughts birth on how next to another we lay
Such victorious teamwork we live out
And it's for that reason, glee filled on mountain top I shout
Having trust in the other causes ongoing blossoming of flowers
This fruitful joy causes myself to stand firm as a steel tower
Just having you causes the rampage of love filling emotions
Onlookers get colored by our forwarding motion
But one thing is known, for body, friendship, character and heart I am the biggest feen
Which is why, have confidence on one can always lean

What was done, to deserve such an in and out beauty
That fact alone, for as long heart beats will dumbfound me
Sweet, special, sexy and superb dynamite knowing you're my teammate will always bring peace
That be the reason you alone have my hearts keys

Our green lands we live is our forwarding school
The partnership we live shines as the footstool
This solo life we live, is used as a teaching tool
The promising future we have guarantees our security
This life together will always color you and me
The unique bridge of harmony our hugs and kisses seal
This unity of love causes the tidal wave of a soul partnering deal
The fabulous enchantment of love encourages us to carry on
Our continuous uplifting comforts all, like the sun

A love as rare as one had doesn't exist
For that alone has me grateful, you I didn't miss
One of a kind is the genuine and pure love built
The so, so passionate and sexual love we have causes me to never do anything at all; which
causes guilt
So, my dear lovable peach, do you yet understand I have nothing but love for the priceless gem
you are
And our forwarding role model behavior only shines bright like the stars
I am definitely always yours
The best life has to offer is all that's desired for my core score
Which is why, as the team day by day our relationship tears down walls and builds bridges of
forwarding
In such the blossoming growth of fruits and greens are rather inviting
That's why my sexy love sickle, the team we are will always prosper
of mine
The fabulously beyond beautiful and one of a kind blessed gift you are, is one who's never tough
to find
And by itself is soul reason, from first breath the home began to take shape
With such, due to your astonished and remarkably creative character I have eternal thanks to
your make

The team we've built ourselves into overcomes all of life's barriers
It's with only you my love I have the earnest desire to for life's length remain merrier and merrier

Sexual teammate it's not possible for myself to have this permanent and unbreakable lock with any other
Within our rooting chemistry the flourishing parade of graceful peace bonds us together stronger and stronger
In the duo partnership we freely live, through the pieced together joyfulness there are times of gleeful light
From one's beaming heart to mine it awakens and shines so, so bright
The great color it is decorates our love making with a symphony of romance
My dear baby, it's that alone I'm tickled through our step-by-step dance
And that my love is why so many look at us and smile
And such love will assist in surpassing any distractions and full of confidence relentlessly travel mile after mile
That my babe, you and I have shaped
It's surely true the love built will last for time of all days

Here we are in this romance the bond life's time has built intensifies as time passes
Sexy love who's each touch blesses the times of relation are enjoyed, because such comforts as we lock and take part in the love inspired dances
These legs will always last
Because what is lived, nothing will ever surpass
There's no possibility for such to be done
Which is why and for me the one and only reason needed my hearts always open and welcoming for you to come

It's just my angel, for who my body hungers
Sexy dessert, better than you it's not possible for there to be any other who even comes close to better
Special love that's the duo we've shaped
Meaning my gift our designed blessing, as one the all-time best package in the step-by-step journey we've formed
A cradled love is what we've birthed
Meaning as the team, our joining rockets shape us into a pleasant filled conjoining
This connection began at birth, which means it required no finding
Therefore, and only due to the permanent lock we've shaped a promising assurance has formed in our heart and spirits
Which always leaves us to having a destination of no limits
Such ground is because we always hold one another stronger than ever

It's also reason I'm always ready to do and claim my full effort in always making sure our foreplay is better
Because you're my woman, past the best reached is our bonding mesh
Our infinite quality which shines obvious and so vividly, is day by day for one another we do nothing bless
These promising tokens which on the day-by-day shine, colors our hearts with knitted together and graceful peace
Yes, my lovable and cuddly yummy delicacy it's with you alone my heart and full drive will always need
Which is because from our first sight of one another began the lock of our joining
And is why it's my greatest hunger and need, myself your always using
Also, reason, you can just know it's with you alone my body constantly thirsts and persistently hungers to feed
That's comes as the soul reason I long to seek out the promises and fruits of our blossoming seeds
My love such also takes rhythm in the steps our forming shares
By which was formed by a joining and devoted care
Therefore, we must use the toys pieced together
It's true when others step to, I don't even bother
And why you can always know it's just with you I long to eat you for all snacks, breakfast, lunch and dinner
So touched I am, we only shine one color, one cord
Therefore, it's with you alone my body wants and needs
Which means my delicious lollipop, it's true there will always be blossoming power in our life awaiting seeds
Such prolongs our teamwork
And will always bond us together, which is because our loving growth works

In times of battling trials, we can always rely on our formed together hands, which shine the teamwork we live, is defiantly no chore
It's in the joy we live which resembles we have the connection stronger and more permanent than ever before
In meaning there will always be such a delicacy of joyful love
It's the beautiful we have which shines the peace of a fragile dove
A time like this, isn't capable for me to define
And does and will always leave me with entire appreciation, you my sexual toy are committed and self can claim you as mine

WE WILL ALWAYS BE TOGETHER

Our friendship will always last
Together, as a team our combination has built a comforting nest
It's you my finish is the secured mean
And dear darling, of your body I'm the biggest feen
Just look in mirror, an awesome in and out beauty
Sexy and special, above the rest blessing there's endless appreciation you chose me
It's true during sleep and when awake, reason you choose glee fills heart
True it is from own spirit to the angels is the love solid dart
Not solo but together the rock-solid bond will always be
Meaning even when arguments standing proud is our well-built tree
There are finishing words our hearts share
By which holds firmness and pushes aside any possible scare
To feel and grasp onto what we have can only be done by us
And that's reason you'll always be my uplifting plus
Key to my heart is you
Which is key and only reason there's no one else to choose
This leaves me with just you as my lifelong teammate
There's complete surety for another my angel I will never trade
Possibility for there to be another who's better does not have any type of existence
To always choose to be one with the beyond beautiful angel just make so much sense
And not only that, meaning your inner full of love glorious beauty, just takes my every breath;
therefore, only possibility I still live is the strength our golden bold is it
Which is reason the variety of tools we've built strengthens the togetherness we live, and causes
the full of loves power as one we limitlessly bring to no limit
Being full of the bond we've built is the steel strengthened friendship our love building does
now and will life's length unbreakably last
Which means the power of the nasty like good times we daily strengthen are spiced as slow,
steady and fast
From birth of the love's togetherness, we live builds us to being unstoppable teammates

By which is the birthed make
Meaning our life's teamwork, as we grow makes us blossom the easily creative sexual positions
And rather tasty &delicious spice to the only flavors myself hungers and are massively delicious
Which blossoms wild orgasms and makes supremely awesome foreplay in what we live, to
having our life's length strength of limitless

And causes me so, from just you desire the day-by-day kiss after kiss
In meaning such has the invincible partnership in us, that grows to limitless height
That alone causes me to always live with delight
Such has me know of you I will never ever live a diet
And gives me our orgasmic might
In meaning babe, I hunger and desire to always hold, just you alone
And my sexy, it's my promise, for life my caused orgasms will make you voice the loudest moans
In meaning my sexy I'm always hungry to hold just you
That makes for life's length there will never be another toy I choose

About you and I, the finish line has no existence
Yes sweetie, I will always desire those sexual lessons; which to my hormones make so much sense
Yes babe, to have another just doesn't have any possibility
Dear love, such appreciation I have that on the daily basis I can see
When thoughts take shape on whether or not to continue, the shape your beauty has brightens
my mind and heart
Reason that comes as the core reason I surely know there will never be another start

In and with me you'll always have grounds for a permanent lie
And such love between one another reaches far past the highest sky
It must always be known, in me love for will wildly always live
It's also reason, in my eyes just you, are the toy who always gives
In meaning my love, there's no other body I desire to lie on
And will always be the confident and our love assured security in keeping you, past what's seen
as the most fun
Because my blessing, it's not possible for there to be any other woman who has any type of
capable possibility of being better
Which continues on shaping, as our steps continuously brings us closer together
I just don't comprehend how there's beauty, then what we've made which has potential of being
exceeded
This truth is our grounds that the lived teamwork has birthed
Therefore, do you yet grasp onto the soul fact it's only you who's my fire, and with such flames
blessings we've made
Which doesn't have to mean young ones, our inspiring friendship soothes and brings realization
that our teamwork shines what we've paved
Ongoing are the positive uplifts our life's shine
Such will always be the needed reason, I'm appreciative you are mine

Now it is and always will be, burning me alive is the fire we've grown

And my dear love, that alone is what our partnership, for me has shown

In meaning the baffled emotions you cause shines light upon our pieced together shipment of love

And is why, when it comes to you nobody will be above

Sweet and sexy doll, it's you alone I desire myself to be with

For life's length it's strived, through any raging waters, sets off is our ship

The intense fire we've built continues to burn down any confronting trials

Which carries us to passing up all distracting miles

The ignoring all mess we live, carries us to limitless grounds

In meaning our bedroom finesse coats the shaped hearts sound

And it's now, we've grown into a complete seal

You to I and I to you is the life lasting deal

Always I'll hold you in my arms

The goal I set out for, is to always be your charm

Baby, your hearts chords are played like a harmonic chord

Precious and beautiful love, are always welcome to come toward

Only you, are heart and minds speed dial

Just you have my devotion to travel endless miles

Meaning sweetie pie, it's with you alone I desire to enter

Truth be told the might of my love can move a planet sized crater

And it's our teamplay which brings me fulfilling warmth

This intense passion only causes my emotions to be uncontrollably firing west, east, south and north

Meaning it's you alone, my sexy blessing I long to live with

And my sexy blessing, as one we are the finish

Hear and now the foreplay and orgasms shape our time together

And has me, when talking about thankful I can state, myself chose her

You alone are my foreplay and sexual toy

Awesome it is to rub and comfort, me you employ

Time together is what makes us stronger shaped

It's you baby, there's appreciation I can claim is one who causes me to willingly lay

Time after time our special times fill me with overflowing joy

In the bedroom is where there's glee, I'm spanked like ones your boy

As times of fulfillment rock my world, priceless measures of satisfaction sexy blessing causes knock me off the edge

It's no surprise our beauty has caused me to fall off the ledge

Meaning love of life, just you have taken it and there's no replacing

Which is why as time passes more secure is our mending

Michael Green

So now love, is it yet comprehended you alone I long to feel
And with just there's fire to strengthen the seal
Meeting you was the blessing all on its own
Feel free to sexually use me, because like the meal I'm not embarrassed to be shown
Yes, sex machine there's longing just you are enjoyed
With such births the growth to be used
In meaning my so adorably precious pie, it's you alone who I daily hunger to enter
Such a fire first birthed with, as a team us being together

YOU ARE
THE SUPREME BEAUTY

In, out and all around, such fabulous love has me your number one fan
From the moment seen, as a lifelong couple was my primal plan
Always in need for more is why for one's touch the hunger will for life be
As my one and only, just you I see
No possible way for there to be sense, on why the beauty like you exists
And is why from your side I will never desire any type of exit

From your heart the beauties undefinable depth births
Using that beauty blossoming fuel, towards mind it heads north
My adorable darling, it is the life lived the truly shines the flavor filling colors, which
innocently marvel
And that beauty alone pleases and soothes
Having such a treasure has me full of content, and surely keeps me from having the blues
Which urges to return and use
That my dear honey sickle is the only reason besides the supreme beauty, another I will not
choose
To exceed your in and out beauty does not have capability to exist
Meaning babe in the only opinion that matters, as the most beautiful your number one on the
y list
Just to know I have will always entirely satisfy me
Which is why one must know on your body myself will always feed
Reason for why, in the loyal partners eyes isn't hard to see
And is reason just you have my hearts key

Topping your supreme greatness doesn't make any possible sense
Which is why for you the love is the most dense
Baby, there's endless appreciation we are the couple
Our beauty is, for one another we are humble
The promising lock which secures our fastened belt
Such brings us so in one another we melt
Meaning sexy blessing I couldn't request any better
That's the core purpose, of you the supreme beauty I strive to always bless her
Having such a beyond beautiful treasure as one's only is the guarantee

There's high appreciation, of how your beautiful self-chose me
So, so fortunate I am, for sure indeed
Just have you realized, it's from no other except you day by day myself feeds
And for one another as comforting love, our bond is the shade providing tree
Such is why, it's on I you can literally always lean
Which is because, it is for your touch I'm the biggest feen
That's right the beyond gorgeous gift, there's no other capable possibility to withhold what's in your ownership; and that's my hearts seed
Owned by, because it's your life that on it, my heart feeds
It is true, for such a supreme beauty my heart bleeds
It's simple to comprehend just how the withheld sparkling beauty knocks aside all of the weeds
Nobody besides you, for entire fulfillment, is the supreme beauty my mind, heart and spirit so direly needs
Appreciation belongs to, that our beauty causes for one another, as the unbreakable and untouchable team we lead
Which is why for just your touch myself has greed
As the team, our lock and bond will last for life, surely
Only your number one beautiful self is who I desire, truly
This fire filling lock we have is the best quality
Besides the supreme beauty, one not better than the other, which means we have life lasting equality
And just knowing you are mine, causes me to morning, day and night party
Yes love, just knowing you chose me has me throw the festivity
Because you just desire me, blossoms every breath revelry
Therefore, the love our teamwork births will always satisfy me
For our honey hive you are the queen bee
Reason your monumental supreme beauty that is it for what I see
Which is it, for why you shine supreme beauty
It's also why, just you are my one and only
Because it's true our togetherness is the most possible healthy
The love who makes me whole, I couldn't ask for anything better
Which is why due to the bond strengthened is our tether
And it is why there's nothing that exists which can disturb our love
Such has no end towards east to west, below and above
Meaning, is it yet comprehended for you my queen there are no limits
That is because for one another there are endless benefits
That love my dear is the token of my life long last
Meaning sweetie pie, our togetherness will always be the awakening blast

My sexy doll, appreciation has presence we not allowed time to pass by fast
My sexy beauty when times are that you're wounded my care is your cast
This love is why the rock-solid bond we've built brings our good times to a permanent lifelong surety
It's founded and built with our friendship's purity
The promising rock we are has the foundation of our love making flowers
I swear babe, in the bedroom it's like you have a beastly power
So therefore, you supremely beautiful work of art it's your beauty by itself, which brings me constant happiness
Therefore, love of my heart, mind, spirit and life for sure only you do and always will bring me endless bliss

I whole heartedly know, there's not another who comes anywhere close to your in and out supreme beauty
And myself feels privileged the beyond beautiful character you shine has been sculpted just for me
There are no words or any type of description, which can possible describe your remarkably outstanding, naughty yet so perfect preciousness
My dear love, easily the most possible beyond beautiful is only you, which is why my angel's nothing less
As way by the farthest and as the greatest possible possibility, from head to toe no lie, easily the sexiest, is your definition
And it's true day by day I'm struck with your untouchable supremely elite, and most emotionally giving beautiful ammunition
Which means dear lullaby the beyond beautiful fire you sport always amazes in such a peace filling harmony
That means my highest possible grade and friendlier than friendly toy, as my one and only, it is just you I see
For such peace to exist, as the supreme beauty there's only one capable possibility, for such to ever be
Which is reason I exist just for you alone, and reason I'm addicted to your supremely beautiful self I know you were made just for me
So, my precious just you are my precious gift you alone are it who has the reserved home in my heart
And my graceful piece of so delicious dessert I'm so geared to have you alone as my finish and start
Yes my precious I'm so greatly in love with your delicate self, I am in complete awe of your supreme beauty
Which is why appreciation and joy flood my spirit and heart, that you alone to open door to my heart have the only set of keys

Michael Green

This my so, so much better than fabulously awesome supreme beauty is why forever we will play
Having hold of one another we'll grasp onto each other till together we entertain each breath;
which will color us; because our foreplay will make tough to entertain that resting day
My beyond supremely beautiful package, inside, out and all around you are easily beyond sexier
than most possible for you to ever be
And that is just in the right now, but bombastic it is reason our day-by-day connection isn't the
only attraction forming the blossoming increase
And naughty doll, I just cannot get enough of the naughty and specially the moans and groans
for more shines that beyond beautiful attraction
My sweet and sexy spanking deserving doll relationship with you, who is way by far easily better
than the best, at the most fire fueled by love have lit on fire each emotion
Yes we are two, but as we have every touch of love the hold of one another strengthens into a
team who is one
And now you be so da crazy on radical and righteously fire torched spank deserving beyond
supremely in charge beyond beautiful
Oh baby, you better believe you are reading the truth, because it be just you who owns my body,
heart, spirit and my love; which day by day in our life's unfolds
That you beyond sexier than sexy and most lively friendly package are the one who has more
than everything I desire
That my sexy package is why of your body, character, friendship and naughtily flavor filled
touch I will never ever grow tired
Of the supremely beautiful loving you feed my heart and mind only hungers to be on the most
possible highest high
My precious doll, when this tidal wave occurs is when we can unleash such a hold that unleashes
bond uniting ignition that through our hormones blasts us to feeling as high as the sky
And now it is we carry each other in such a hold which embraces and secures a more
strengthened than iron solid lock
With our shaping through the formation of emotions we shape each-others hearts using our
friendship shaped blocks
Baby girl, you are it, for who I want to enter, and just your especially sexy self is who myself
massively hungers to feel and kiss
The most possible fabulously extreme best possible gift you are, and blessing like no other it's
not possible to comprehend the appreciation I have that you I didn't miss
So sweet and special love like no other there are no words which can describe the uncontrollable
festive fire loving the supreme beauty has lit
It's true between one another has formed the love strong and friendship solid our bonds steel
strong kit
My love it's true, between us the togetherness we've formed will always live as our hugging hold

— 148 —

And that my adorable was, is, and always will be our friendship built with back-and-forth love strong mold

Hear we are and our connection will be life-long; for in you, and within I lives the conjoining caress of our hands, lips, bodies and spirits

Which means, between our locking togetherness there will for our life's length be no possible limit

Yes girl it's true, reason love between two is the reason there is life, and keeping that belief does cause us to maintain the hold of one another

Because my love there isn't any possibility for me to besides you ever hunger the lock with any other

Which is because there's just one and only one beauty who can ever be that possibility for the one, I choose

And sweetie pie that solo rose who is full of supreme beauty only has possibility of being the supreme beauty; and you are the one I sexually abuse

That is why, on my life my life's goal is to for life's length as my hearts key to day by day only have one the one supremely beautiful gift; as the one I use

These grounds mean preciously adorable love, reason you desire just myself, for life's length as having the all-around most gorgeous I will never lose

There are so many times I see you and because my hormones explode a chubby begins and eyes focus on what my thoughts see is due

Which is why, as my one and only supreme beauty I whole heartedly only have capability to always state, I love you!

It's not possible for there to anyone better than the sweet, adorably precious and beautifully sexy blessing

Baby girl, it is your beyond beautiful love I am not deserving

Which is the reason it's not possible for there to be any understanding to just why you find me interesting

My sweet and sexually glamorizing pearl your every touch is my fire and's definitely in the most pleasurably uplifting

Such means my honey sickle there isn't anyone coming one bit close to your monumental and supremely beautiful greatness

And reason I desire the best, I've won, because you are nothing less

That baby is the key reason, it's only you who is, fabulously marvelous, and desiring any other makes no sense

Sweetly precious love, what's been built is love dense

Even though we've argued, the priceless art one is causes your supremely beautiful self to ongoingly bless me, until I am content

The endless priceless jewels our relationship makes is meant

Meaning we live just to please one another
Because of such passion's why there's appreciation myself can comfortably state, 'as my one and only I have her'

Tidal waves roar with your presence
Just beauties your essence
Just where you began; my dear there's no possible explanation
Sexy blessing just with you alone is the only possible destination
To kiss you is the only goal I desire to meat
Diving deep and to taste, is the additional treat
Sexy blessing, always when low it's on my shoulder you can lean
It's true, for your body I'm the biggest feen
What's within your heart and mind's explosively attractive and are the central attraction I never want to be without
Meaning my fragile and beautified genuine art are one of a kind, for is the gift I will always stand proud and shout
In my eyes your physical beauties remarkably astounding but my dear it's that inner which conquers and is why for another I'll never push you off that reef
That's reason as my remarkably supreme beauty your heart and mind play part of being easily the loving and friendly chief

Cannot even wish for better than what you are
Or make up the better package, than you my star
As you are present dumbfounded thoughts begin to shape
It's in the bedroom, you're the monkey and I'm the ape
These colors ignite the passionate love we live out
Reason we're side by side equals, we are the chief and the day-by-day life's we shine is our scout

Do you yet comprehend, besides you there's no possibility to be the most beautiful
That's why your very life's so majestically colorful
Meaning the superb beauty, you are decorates me with pieced together blessings
Bewildered is my minds state, because I can look for reason on why you have supreme beauty but am always going to be seeking

NO ONE'S
BETTER
THAN

Never thought one would be found like
For you precious, I'm present for all hikes
Yes baby, of course I'm always satisfied
Girl the beauty alone leaves me mystified
At just how artwork, such as yourself even exists
Which leaves me as the one who never desires to exit
The profound greatness has me unable to find the right words
But my sexy blessing, it is on the beauty's heart, which exist those perfect cords
It's for that reason it's known I have the best possible
Also, why you're stunning self well passes profoundly incredible
Meaning dear, because we've overcome so much, for me there's just cannot be another
Which results with the only truth, because I have you and desire the best, there's no possible
capability of me having any other

In such a graceful melody, love streams throughout your body
Reason day by day life, with glorious peace ones heart richly colors me
Such shaping takes place, throughout our daily achievements
Reason your far better than max, life will have to cause chaos to make any dents
What we've built has the strongest lock, between our hearts
And has myself know, I'll never need another start
Here we are and as time passes the hunger to embrace and continue love-based devotion only
increases
Yes babe, massively better than best possible entirely pleases
There's no stop to your oncoming blessings, which is because of the complete package you've
grown into
I will always be thankful we've formed into one; from the beginning of two
Which is why it's not possible there'll ever be another to choose
And baby, such flows out in always desiring myself is a victim of sexual abuse
It can always be in know, in bed and life I'll always be present to use
For that you can have surety there'll never be any excuse
Which seals the deal to our lock

The fastened hold clasps onto our heart's cords, which is why from I'll never walk
That means my blessing besides you there's not any other who's fuel to my heart
This comes in meaning, your awesomely supreme and so over the top self can't be put on any chart
In meaning our teamwork is the guaranteed passage way
And is why, besides one another we are destined to lay
It's besides each other we will always live fulfilling happiness
The beyond beautiful package of love is what's desired, and with you I got nothing less

There's no possibility, because your beautiful self has entirely pleased me
It just cannot be done, better than you is a unknown sum
To hold, kiss, rub and love does and always will catapult me, to an unknown land of mystical candies
It's you babe who my heart beats for, by which has me know that are the best possible score
And the moment when I comprehend that is your best, you hit me with a over the top finish
Happiness is all you deliver, which is the core reason I'll always brag the grade A I have her
Stars twinkle in your eyes and joy dances throughout your heart, which is why my dearest love thanks will always be, that you gave me the start
Unable to calculate just why your beauty never fades, the only possible reason that has sense is the day-by-day friend you are leaves me in a maze
Our rock-solid partnership brings us together as one unit, which causes our teamwork to have no possible limit
And it's during those times, that we fall deeper into one another's hold, and is why with another I never want to mold
Myself is happy and content with you, so girl you never fear there will be another I choose

For you to improve is why it's known that day will never possibly exist
Just know girl, from your side there'll never be an exit
It's now that time has stopped, reason there's no understanding on just where and how a gem like you took shape
Where the beyond beautiful blessing you are is from isn't known, or just what is your make
All I know is there just cannot be a better gift than what we've mend
Or how your inner and outer beauty shaped, and comprehension to why the oncoming has no end
There just has to be a cause to the life of love you live, and the peace you shine in the daily journeys
Such grounds catapult me to new finding
Always at a lose of words, and knowing not to what is before my eyes
But baby, there just has to be a reason to the continuous blossoming of beauty within you

And the overpowering mixture of ticklish love and naughty sex just empowers me to know I'm
right; with who
There are no words which can possibly define your impeccable love
Such grace always leaves me at a parade of emotions, and has me know it's not possible to be above
In meaning you girl are my one and only and without, just makes no possible sense
That's right, what we've built has unbreakable dense
It is together that when our wings intersect
Such a connection builds our web of naughtiness and secures our net
As we hold each other our times of romance blossoms such memorable love
By which causes me towards all the other offers, towards the trash haul off and shove
Your so better than over the top, it's understood that you aren't able to cope with the most
fabulous elite in and out beauty your glamour shines
A blessing it is, because tasting you is intake of the rarest and most royal wine
My gifts for you do not come close to what you are worth
There's no possibility to define the depths to you, who is the premium score
Meaning girl, it's only you who is my obsession
Because, when discussing better than the rest you I always mention
Being entirely satisfied with what we are, is me to the fullest
And baby as we grow our partnership will just better our nest
Which is why, it's you alone who has a home in my heart
Sweet and sexy babe, it's you alone who always rockets me north
There is so much about you that fulfills me
Sweet love, it is true you alone have and own my hearts keys
So, my dear love, you alone have a surety
And it's now that I'll always put you before me
Meaning you my sexy lollipop, one lick is never enough
And during those bedroom spells you dish out, I can never keep hush
That token always has me feel like I'm getting the plus
This fuel is the fire that causes me to always feed my must
In meaning it's just you who is my gift
And the one who always gives me that needed lift
Which is why, it's you who causes me to roll over the top and always know I'm the victor
The individual who has the cupid who's better than the rest, and has me always feel like the one
who has the perfect score
My sweet and adorable love, do you yet understand it's only, who is the best possible treat
Just look at who you are, and just how you are so exquisitely neat
There are times of joyful glee, that color what our tree
Knowing I have the best in you, is known by me

Michael Green

Now it is time that we hold one another close, and pour our hearts out to each
In doing so is why, as humble as one can be, for you I'm down on my knees

Just look at what you and I have built
The shape we are, so strong prevents any guilt
Our foundation is so strong and untouchable are our heights
Such grounds have me know that for me, you are right
Honey sickle, it is true for my day by life you alone are my light
The beyond beautiful blessing you are, shines so bright
For such grounds to form required our loyal devotion
Yes babe, appreciation is mine which is because you as my friend causes wild emotions
These feelings take me to a new level
From your heart to mine is a love thickened funnel
Yes, sweetie the union we share carries us to grounds which have never been explored
Making it for just two, to be toured
By doing such shines our flavored colors
In meaning this land is just for you and I and no other
So baby, it is now that we enchant times of flavoring within our spirits
And such brings us to a peak of no limit
These tickles enchant us for upcoming days
It's also reason with complete ease, being love bridged beside one another we lay
Happiness flows from me to you, and the same in return; which will carry us hand by hand till
the last breathes we do
Yes dear, my sweetly yummy and sexier than all other unique gift, because I'm treated with
myself never wants a new
There might be many more, but I wouldn't like any other to choose
Because you are mine, I always have top of the line; who's at my use
In our times of forwarding passion, our trust in each shoves aside all distractions
Definite gratitude, that I found you is mine
Reason be babe, I'm sure that you are top of the line
And girl it's the guarantee I cannot get any better
The beauty which is beaming from who you are tickles me with all the weathers
And that's just your inner beauty, by which means the coating of romantic love harnesses our
bond with a solidly firm outlasting
By which causes me to always see and use and never overlook and be passing
Which is reason it's just you who has me at a loss for words
These times are why, besides you I would like no other cord

— 154 —

So, my dearest and most beautiful love, do you yet grasp onto the beyond beautiful blessing you are

So fragile you are, such shines bright like the stars

Because it's easy for me to comprehend, your friendliness, thoughtfulness, caring, loving and I'm delighted as we bend

Our giving relationship strengthens our tree, it's collected, throughout our unique tokens of collective unity

Our bond will always keep us as a secured lock, and will assist us in strengthening our tree

Baby, who is my unique love, it's just you I desire to always enter and firmly hug

With no other is my only hunger, so my sexy we are destined to be one, forever

It is just you who I see as the top prize, and my dear sexy choosing you, for me was so wise

Tender is our embracing, and honey for that time all day I'm fantasizing

And being with you love is one and only desire, which is why just you are on the unbreakable and permanent hire

Just look at your sexy self, which is there's a spot just for you on the top shelf

Being without you is massive misery, that's why I've classified you and know you're the prize who always makes me happy

Such awareness will always cause me to long for your body, and there's nothing else I desire to be within me

Your naughtiness excites, and furthers your ongoing light

My babe, it's you alone who pleases, and dear gorgeously sexy I get thrilled, because you are the one who teases

Just you are the one I long to lick, and it's only your head-to-toe body as the one who is the high-grade pick

There just cannot be another who comes close, which is why it's solely you my grade A prize, I choose

And wrapping my arms around your body, brings me so much joy, which is why for our life's length just you are my gorgeous sex toy

And now is when myself comes before you and just begs for your touch, babe, that is right just who you be, is desired so, so much

My dear love you just don't understand the sacred prize you have grown into, just spending time with my blessing has self-know the one and only for me, my beauty is you

The play we do, fulfills me to full, and those times of our one-on-one excitement satisfies my goal

Yes, to bring you over the top orgasms puts me on a new level, therefore my day-by-day mission comes in awarding your in and out beauty the most precious metals

And how I do such is the guarantee I shine throughout our understanding, meaning love of life there's not any other possibility of one to have the key you use for access to my singing

Yes honey, through my spirit I sing within your heart, in such grounds is why, in all ways for more of you I'm on board for the new day start

Because sweetie it's just you I long for, and that's the core reason for my blessing there always be an open door

In these times of happiness is when I long and hunger, making me state, 'I desire no other than you as her'

In the times of absent of, tremendous degree of downfall causes me to miss my dove

That's right babe, in and out you cause me to appreciate another day

More time with is it, as my core desire, baby, I am totally for sure of you I'll never grow tired

So, sweetie pie it's now time that we build our heart stronger, and in doing so as one we color one another with our heart's feathers

Therefore, sexy candy, just allow me to throughout the day and night snack on body

Because that's what entirely fulfills, meaning communication and all types of foreplay and naughtier and beautiful it is our time has overcome all the hills

Therefore, and meaning I can't cope on living without our relationship, it is the guarantee for me you were sent

And that's why on me, you can always lean

And you've proven as the friend I can always count on you, which proves I was wise in who I choose

Meaning I'll never turn my back on or push away, and point is my arms will always be open for you to lay

Such means girl it is I who desires no other except you, and besides, desires nobody new

Therefore, we can be stronger in the hold of one another, and the taste of each is and always be the most delicious custard

My dear sexy, I'm entirely pleased with you

Which is why in the bedroom I always want to be the one who's sexually used

Meaning my sweet, sassy, naughty and incredibly delicious candy what is mine I never want to lose

So special one feels, because your appreciative character has me always feel upbeat and new

Therefore, pleasurable delight as one it's easily known our bond will overcome all fights

In meaning you, the one and only adored treasurable sweetening dessert my eyes are geared towards no other except the one who gets all my sexually might

It is only you, that my heart, spirit, body and mind longs for

Just thoughts of you, to my me are the crazy like treasure

With your name stitched in, day by day I beat peaceful passion

Such wild like warmth the touch of you, brings my body

Which is why, as one you will never lose my spirit and me

The invisible matters, because your bodies known, so therefore there will always be satisfying delight

In meaning sexy candy our hearts fine tune will always keep up on our life length flight

Which means our teamwork carries one another to new grounds

And has us in a rhythm, of just our own sound

This is when we come together and take off, with a new vision intact

Us being one, is the exact

Meaning my adorably precious dessert, as we work more and more together there'll always be awesome unity

So, do you yet realize the beyond perfect team is you and me

With this placement of unbreakable teamwork, as one we will always hold each other closer and closer

Which is why, I'll always have one and never need another

No room for a new turn

Because I desire and have in my heart the best churn

My dear beyond beautiful blessing you are it for what my mind and heart desires

And of your character, I'll never grow tired

So tasty, there's no way I ever could

And surely, I never should

The better than best possible gift, only possibility for you to be

Which verifies together the seeds we produce will build strength to our tree

In meaning you're the best for me, and I am for you

That sum tells us wisdom was present in the what we choose

THE MOST FABULOUS LOVE

Of you, myself can never get enough
The beauty is, reason we achieve tasks as a team, not one obstacle is tough
Such a enjoyable blessing it is, that your character and body are over the top
Sweetie, it can be relied on that from my heart you'll never drop
Dear bombastic babe, your taste always has me earning for some
And during those naughty times, the fabulous touch given creates the best possible cum
It is easily comprehended, my beauty delivers the most flavorful fun
The best of the better than, defines my adored hun
Just holding you in arms is a flavor that's longed for, and the hunger one feeds from
When we're together, of that complete package love I yearn for more; than just some
Our life's only have success in the geared determination
In meaning, as one there's nothing which will cause any deformation
For our joy, from hearts to lips our happiness flows
And within the ongoing life's our togetherness lives, such shows
Here we are, and as our love is we shine ongoing friendliness
Which is the assured guarantee to always bring us endless bliss
It is, that always we will have the permanent last
So beautiful it is, our steady selves graciously love and nurture one another; making sure to
meet that right spot, at not to fast
In and out has the romancing melody
With such tender grace, blossoms the majestic harmony
It's now my love, that you're held tight within my arms
Most fabulous love, sweet and sexy baby are and will always be the hearted charm
Meaning sweetie, I can never be without you
Which means I'm only left with one to choose

In and out of bed, I'm left with nothing except the best
Therefore, besides the highest grade I have nothing less
Meaning there's no more question to it or wondering on if, my sexy charm is the best possible
love and the only desired body
That has definition of, just my gift is the one and only desired candy
Sexually and emotionally, you're uplifting
And it's the guarantee, when in need if not by mouth through heart, your love's always
complimenting
Better than couldn't be dreamed of or wished for

That's known because fire for lives within my heart, as the true score
This means, no other except from head to toe it's just your body I desire
For you sexy, I'm always ready to hire
So awesome it is, I'll never grow tired of that touch
Because it is, the key myself craves, so much
Therefore, it's now easy to understand why I'm crazy in love with the most fabulous
Reason for that beauty, still to this day is seen as miraculous
Needing more, I always am
Which is because, quit easily I'm your number one fan
The truth is simple for one to comprehend
We are meant, because in troublesome times, for one another our bond mends
Destined is our hearts as one
Complete love is our built sum
The teamwork we live blossoms day-by-day flowers
And in return, with graceful peace our spirits enjoy showers
As time passes a beautiful rhythm of firm yet fragile river of elegant beauty holds us
unbreakably together
Within our fastened love, delicacy coats as it's tickled with the most beyond beautiful and
gorgeously colored feathers
Dear darling, it's your pieced together heart, that has my addiction
You sweetie are the cause of my high wired emotions
As a team we carry one another throughout the tough times
The partnership shared blossoms throughout our playtimes
For, there's not enough thanks
To endure, follows the spanks
What's been built will always have the guarantee
Which took birth from what's was designed by you and me
In meaning, in our togetherness we shine fabulous love
Such joy travels from yours to my heart, and assists in feeling above
The birth of our partnership builds the surety of the lasting hold
Bettering us is our untouchable and lasting mold
Piece by piece, as we've grown our hearts were sown together
And so rock solid the love we share is, all distractions do not even bother
The great wall, which held together by our relationship
Through our adventures and journeys, onto one another we have a strong love-built grip
Reason the complete package one is, to endlessly please is my mission
Day by day I intend on giving, as my mission
With just you, as my one and only is my orchestra

Which is why, to you it will always make sense to sing, I love ya
Meaning my sweet and sexy babe, there just cannot be any better
You can count on me, look at me as your cozy sweater
Reason I'll always be there, you'll never feel alone
And it's together, meaning in one another's arms we'll always feel home

Thanks to, https://s/photos/the-word%2C-love

I'M FULFILLED

Reason you're my sweetie, satisfied I am
Such ticklish humor overflows, as smiles leave me as your number one fan
I am so lucky; you claim me as your property
For you my honey sickle I'm down on my knees
In full there's nothing except pleasure
My love for, cannot be measured
You babe are the satisfying token; which I'm determined to never lose
And there's thankfulness, it's I you've abused
Absolutely there's no doubt in my emotions for you
Such genuine fruits forward our bond
Reason I'm at your beckon call's why you can classify me as your pawn
No other flavor than you are stimulating fulfillment; no other font
In meaning my delightful treat, because you're better than anyone else
Which is why my fire ignites when you let just rip off your blouse
That means dear love, it's your tongue I crave to lick my penis
Such excitement follows and shall send me to the peak of limitless
Yes, my sex machine there are no distance I wouldn't travel for you
That precious love is why it is you I do and will always choose

Colorful candy is what enchants my mind
This treat happens to be, because in and out you are so fine
Nothing touches the overflowing fulfillment you are
That dear is reason you are my star
It's nice I can count on, you are never far
You are right on track, a spot for my angel is always number one on my chart
As time passes such journeys, we embark upon
My satisfaction soars high because your lips cause relief as I cum
In such flavors of rockets engulf my never-ending satisfaction with you
And is why I appreciate it is me, as the only man you use
Listen to my sweet whispers
To, is such pure commitment there's surety I'll never miss out on her
So rambunctiously over the top fun is the bond we chart
Therefore, you being my friend is like healing to any scars
Which is why without you makes no sense
And has no grounds for any finish

Here I am, and there's no other peak that's desired to reach
Your pussy juice is the milk and body is the meat
Content I am, that your looking stopped with me
As that special one, because you're my friend it wasn't hard for me to see
As time passes my engulfing doesn't stop, of that which gracefully strokes the chords of my heart
This sweet and so superb flames torch my yearning for lips of love
And has me just know your beauty has innocence; like that of a dove
That means luscious love you are it, for my one and only
There's no capability for there to be another; no possibility
It's my promise babe you will never feel alone
From my spirit to yours is the one-way phone
On and in is where I desire to lye
Now and for our life long journey, my love will never be in any disguise
I mean, my thoughts are consumed by unique character
I'm consumed by the love we share, & that's reason there's appreciation myself has ground to
claim, I found her
Reason you, I only move forward
Always sexy dear, I always lean toward
As looked at, beyond beautiful blessings seen
Great thanks exist, because we are destined to further our tree
And our fruit is not just that which blossoms upon
Special and delicious candy, in your direction I will always come, come
But that which prospers from our day-by-day life
The ongoing love I'm feed is the cure to any strife
Sexy baby, sit and feel that which coats with friendliness
With warming tickles, and fulfilling love brings me such bliss
There's nobody I'd rather kiss, hug, all types of touch and love
There is no other better than, not any other above
I cannot find any description that explains how pleased I am
My entire satisfaction has me as your number one fan
This joy has me with you be so glad
So calming are your sparks, during stressful times I just cannot get mad
Such a satisfying joy you are
Happiness lives within, and relationship with you has healed all the scars
These promising grounds has me know choosing you was smart
Which always causes endless fruit to blossom within my heart
And it's why I know you as mine was the wisest choice
Our bond causes confidence in knowing together we have one voice

Choosing wasn't a questionable decision
Until I have, naming you as my key love is my only mission
Meaning babe, when it comes to you there's no other to choose
Reason why morning, day and night by, I long to be used
Within body I yearn to be intertwined
And your sassy juice tastes like a out of world wine, and is reason day by day it's desired
Because of the graceful heartbeats, which pitter patter, ongoingly tickling of a steady pace has
its presence
Reason my addiction it's easy for one to know between us there will never be any kind of fence
So, baby it just cannot be fathomed on how such an in and out beauty like you has any chance
of existing
There's no possible sense on where you are from
So true it's you're within roses flourish with a delightful taste; like that from a plum
I don't comprehend on just how a beautiful blessing such as yourself even exists
And sexy the withheld in and out beauty's so great it makes no sense to be any list
Which is why, day by day to feel and kiss is my mission
To me, such honor's felt it's like in order to kiss I need permission
On me, I desire just your body to be laminated
And my tongue craves the sweet, sweet taste, which has never faded

All the bells and whistles, in full are filled
You, my dear babe is my addictive pill
And just holding your hand is by far beyond the best possible gift
The awesome plus is you're easily better than the best lift
In my eyes, it's not even possible for me to comprehend the beyond beautiful blessing you are
So fabulously great is your in and out kindness, your heart shines bright like the nighttime stars
And it's wise to be confident in my hold
Because it is true, just for you is the within mold
I feel so lucky to have you, as my heartthrob
I will treat you as my angel; because I don't want any other to rob
Meaning girl, it's for there will always be open hands
As we lay it's desired, I sink within, like one in quicksand
Reason your character I constantly have times of overflowing joy
Which is reason there's craving to be used like a toy
Those naughty times excite me with bombastic fire
And is reason, of your heart, mind, friendship and body I will never grow tired
So baby, for me to grasp onto what your rhythmic beat is I'm at a loose of words
Which is why, if depression knocks thoughts of you rocket me north

So my love, appreciation I have for our bond
And is why, I just know you are my fawn

There you are, as beautiful as ever could be
Such treasures not only are your face, but your body glistens such special roses and pansies
Which is why it's just not understood why you choose me
How such a gift as yourself even sees myself as worthy
It is true, for you and you alone love like no other can ever exist
Baby, that is why it's my life's goal, from my heart you never miss
And I just know, precious peach is why I will never exit
In our love, I have crazy confidence
Because sweetie pie, in you are the keys to my heart
And is reason with you I will never have another start

Thanks to, https://images.unsplash.com/photo-1588599038109-34894258f69b?ixid=MnwxMjA3fDB8
MHxwaG90by1wYWdlfHx8fGVufDB8fHx8&ixlib=rb-1.2.1&auto=format&fit=crop&w=889&q=80

I have ongoing naughty dreams of you
Such evidence has me know, who I did was wise one to choose
These constant nighttime pleasures could also be reasoning your sweet face is always on mind

That's why babe, it's comprehended you're the best possible find
Within you is such beyond beautiful peace
My honey bun I can't say it enough how appreciative I am you stick with me
I mean so beautifully crafted is your body
With you my precious is where I always want to be
Baby. In my eye's self resembles a beauty that pleases
Such a bodies loved, all shapes and creases
In my eyes, which is all I care about such a beautiful piece of fragile and beautifully pieced
together art
Who is and always will be far, far beyond #1 on my chart
Then, will be, there and here in the now I so greatly hunger you
Which has me confidently know you're the one to choose
So adorably sexy are your smiles, I just cannot get anything better
And in our mold, I am the base, we are the structure and our makings beautified as its colored
with your lovely feathers
I could not ask to have our romance with any other than you
Sweet, sweet baby there are just no words which describe my sexual love; and that baby knocks
aside all deceptive words which try to turn me from and confuse
So, my so sexy present, I need you to whole heartedly and with all your mind have and always
keep in and out trust in me
It's been lived and now with all love filling emotions. day by day I am enriched by what I've
unlocked with your hearts key
1And reason you have me glued to, daily I pass by all other attempts to distract
But its easy to ignore, which is reason it's known I have the best; to the exact
Meaning now my sweet, special, sexy and supremely fulfilling peach, who I have is why I'm
content
Reason the satisfaction, I just know, us as one is definitely meant

Within our connection are rainbows of love, which shower us both with impeccable beauty
And baby, reason your ongoing life such is easy for me to see
Meaning my dear love, it's you sweetie who's desired to be with
It's also reason, now and it'll always be I desire only you as my finish
And it's easily known, the tenderness within does not want to be missed
Also is why there is eternal appreciation that for just once I can claim you as the one, I've kissed
So marvelous you are, it just can't be fathomed how you even exist
It's easy to comprehend, your beauty cannot be put on any list
Far to great, which has any classification
You definitely are sweet, special and a sexual sensation

Which is reason, in and out you are the beyond beautiful blessing
Just look in the mirror and evaluate life and you know, it's not possible for me to be messing
Within you are the furthering flowers of positivity
And that's where the fired flames of love carry me
It is now my love, within day-by-day life I have rest in knowing I am yours and you are mine
Sexy love, I just know that you were, are and always be easily top of the line
And through our ongoing relationship that's comprehended in full
It's still, and always will be accurate, there will never be anything that comes any bit of close to your special class
So perfectly special, in my eyes your in and out structure always will be
Such appreciation is withheld that you've chosen self to be the one who on you lean
Fiene is your satisfying body and cheer filling spunk
And my hungered blessing, reason your mine I have the victorious slam dunk
Hear we are and as life's wheel keeps turning the joy between builds stronger
Listen hear my delicious popsicle, ongoingly I dance thanks; reason you I can proudly state, 'I have her'
It's an all-day and night thing, quite self is
Which is reason it be you is who I never want to miss
Within there is one gear to never lose premise
Of that which keeps me stuck on every beat
That my dear assists my step-by-step feet
In meaning the passion to live is ignited by your fire
It's true, of you, I will never grow tired
Which is because of such a genuinely pieced together art I literally am dumbfounded
Such a dynamite friendship we've built causes appreciation we've founded
To express how entirely fulfilled I am will never make sense
Even to describe the ongoing journeys of thrill you cause isn't possible for me to express
Baby, it's you I live for and heart is always smiling
Which causes gratefulness it's you I will never state, I'm missing
So especially beautiful delight, just know I'm always at a loss for words
Reason your sexy body, with naughty passion uncontrollably beating are my hearts cords
I mean girl, just spending time with you rockets me north
Before you I'm humbled, which is why you have the respect of saying, come forth
In is such infamous angelic beauty, which shines bright in your every step
That is why, for just one hug at any time I will climb from the deepest depth

So adorably superb love of life, it's you who's longed to care for
And with, I strive in tending to any needs and inhibiting all soars

Reason because there's nothing else that can possibly be any better
Also, reason there's enjoyment in claiming, for, selves at end of a tether
At any given time, when you call, I'll fulfill ones needs
It's for your touch, my heart bleeds
Entirely I'll always have thanks you exist
For that is another reason there's appreciation I did not miss
And for that causes love filled rivers to stream heart to heart
It's also reason appreciation I have you gave me that start
Not mattering who asked, through the hills and valleys you remain with me
Which verifies my know and confirms what I see
Here we are, as happy as ever could be and in such a love the bountiful presence of glee enriches
our coming and going
It's yesterday we laughed and today, for our lock the love keeps on pushing
Being feed by the friendship we share, such a permanent stamp of approval we have for each other
My dear lovable blessing, better than, it's not possible to be another
Which is the primal reason why, I'll always be yours and have undefinable thanks you are
my cover
And any sideshows which try to distract, towards those I don't even bother
Reason it is only you who has that key, and just you who I will always keep
Fueled by love, I'm rubber cemented, therefore, for any other I'll not leap
My in all area emotions, are uncontrollably on fire and have no containable height or
definable depth
Such is also reason there's massive appreciation you with me, as you do every breath
Meaning my love, it's you day by day I long to enter
For baby, the great happiness we share fulfills and in such, our journeys carry us from one step
to another
The ongoing tokens of fateful promises between hold us as one
For our words constantly bring forth our ongoing love
And will always shine the innocence of a beyond beautiful dove
Our surety will keep us as a team forever
And through our one-on-one time. It's easily understandable we'll be together
Our life as one holds the promising fate of a blessed story
My love, it's true the guarantee is your shaping and my seed
So, honey sickle I am and always will be true to the colors we share
It's during our naughty times, ongoingly I feel at the fair
And reason I feed for when you are that hungry teddy bear
Meaning you my beyond beautiful gift can be light and gentle but on other hand load your guns
and your hunger for sexual pleasure doesn't care

By which means you have no thoughts besides getting my dick in your pussy

That my out-of-control sex feen, much, much more than pleases me

So, my sex machine, that's reason all attributes and qualities about you fulfill my passion

Which is why to satisfy what completes is my core and only function

And it's true you sit on my lap and rest on chest, and sexy doll such comforts enjoyed as my heart beats within

You see sweet cheeks, we are the package deal, meaning you're inside me and baby, within spirit and mind, I'm in

Meaning it's now and forever such passionate rivers of love run from me to you, and vice versa

Here is where we are, and I try my hardest but have nothing that can compete with ya

Your inner beauty, which pours from your heart and all around it completes

And yes, it's true dear such life one lives entirely satisfies me

Meaning love of my life, there are just no words which can come even the smallest bit of close, to defining my love for you

Girl, day by day I question myself, why is it me you desire to use

Oh yes, my love the time is upcoming more and more blessings will blossom

With such you'll invite with words, come, come, oh yes, my sex come, come

I'm definitely not complaining, how hungry you are for my love

You do and will always have me

And that's not hard to see

One of a kind is our teamwork

Which is sourced, when I'm hungry you are my pork

Day by day I feed on your body and within such, the heart is yearned for

And to achieve and keep is definitely no chore

Meaning in and game is my want and will

And baby, your body is so ill

Which means it satisfies and pleases; in all ways

That comes as reason, it's together we'll be for all of days

Meaning my dear love, there's not one single thing which can get in the way of the connection that lasts

Our pace of shared beat by beat isn't slow or fast

It relaxes and has a steady rhythm

My sexy doll, this has reason, you're the bosom

Up there you are above the most beautiful angel

And your sexy spirit, self, mind and skin is so yummy and gentle

How can your mind, seriously girl who you are puts me on a new level

When I'm down, you babe color heart with beyond beautiful flowers

Which has myself feel like the highest tower

It's in such the mystical and passionate enjoyment the drive to continue on hungering; then feeding plays itself a specialized and delightful song

Between us, our lovely emotions travel like a pong

Here we are, and as we peer into others eyes, such a tickling romance blossoms a comforting potion

To you and you alone, has my complete devotion

Dedication and loyalty to just you have my entire commitment

And it's now you must understand, there will never be another

Better than the farthest possible, dear beyond beautiful gift you quit easily are

In and out, you have the highest score

Which is why loving, is and never will be any type of chore

Hey babe, we are always to be and will enjoy life-long last

And girl through our relationship, in making sure it's exactly right I'll never take us fast

That's my reason you sexy are my fulfilling pleasure

Also, why it's just you who be my finessed treasure

Sweet and special babe, with my licking enjoyment I can taste, within your heart and mind are mysterious riches

That's reason just you are my one and only finish

Because it's true just your body I desire and strive to finesse

I mean my love just look in the mirror, for it is in my heart and eyes your heart, mind and body is definitely not in any type of mess

So sweet and sexy blessing, reason I have the luscious pearl, then the best I have nothing less

Which is why it's my desire to feel your skin as I rub it or so delicately cares

While I massage with hands and tongue which bring you endless pleasure

And within such I sooth or tickle my blessings skin with my penis like feather

And precious you'll always have a home in my heart and mind

Which is because, besides you I desire no other kind

Meaning just you is it for who I desire to lie on

And with awakening it's you my sweet dear who is my beyond beautiful fawn

And yes, upon your heart so delicately my kisses color

Which reveals, I am your devoted lover

In this climb together, for as long as we live

And for you to enjoy, day-by-day the full effort I give

In a rhythmic passion and with naughty sexual playfulness such pieced together enjoyment is why I will always be yours

Meaning, there's no chance or room for any more

Therefore, is it yet understood just your lips, legs, breasts, face and heart are my one and only score

It's true, when it comes to you, being game to fight for or endure any hard times does not phase me; in any way
Reason such outlasts all other times of troubling days
Do you yet comprehend, it's just, meaning you alone who will ever have any chance of success or play
This has concrete ground, by which means there's only room for you alone
And such colors in meaning, there are no other possibilities for there being another who I would phone
Such comes with direct purpose in the delicious taste of fragrant fruits
Which guides myself on the pathway for that blessed loot
These keys of marvelous fortune always direct me towards genuine treasures
This delight causes myself to realize my love for you, by far pasts any measure

Thanks to, https://images.unsplash.com/photo-1495001258031-d1b407bc1776?ixlib=rb--rop&w=334&q=80

Myself is entirely satisfied with your body
In and out, which means all in all it's you babe who is the hottest beauty
My so precious and sexy pearl it's your hearts gold which tickles and enchants
And baby, there's nothing better than being your man
That day, long ago my eyes caught taste of your characters glee
And since then, I just knew yourself is my hearts key
My precious pearl, it's you sweetie day by day I long to kiss
And just having privilege to hold you I never want to miss
So my so sexy and adorable peach, it's only you my lips hunger to feel
And is why for you, on that day, I'll never be ashamed myself kneeled

About Author

Following achieving the basics and proper procedure of word placement, my Teammates were used. Not with human friends because every so called one from the well popular, Rogers class of 01, and even though I was crazy popular Emerald Ridge class of 04; when not face to face I got the finger.

When, South Hill had my residence I took it upon myself to quit often visit, local mall. That's when people of all ages and professions were conversed with, and doing such built my knowledge on how the woman likes to be treated and feed me growth on what pleases.

Realizing I had the capability to see in the Spirit I was feed insight to catch the state of a person. If there's anyone who desires verification from someone who can be trusted either ask, Puyallup police officer, Ken Hill or Deputy Cary from South Hill sheriff. Why? Before their names were spoke, I feed both of those coo cats insight about themselves, I shouldn't know.

Now for the rocky side. Meaning while being in a wheelchair everyday life hasn't been easy. People from my immediate and moderate family, and all except one, Jakobe=AAA (02, 03) the seventeen caregivers from, AAA, ten from, Good to be Home and four from state have either verbally abused me, stolen or ruined my stuff. Covering those three subjects there's just two people I've forgiven. There was no apology with words but their life and how they treated me afterwards revealed that they were sorry.

Besides the, emts, Bill Cunningham: brunette, Isaac Knots: red head, Highline doctors, Dr. Wuss: man, Dr. Mary: woman, and Dr. Stevens: man the worst was my sister, Britany R. Ortega and her ex, Duryea Coleman. Because four times they stole my sports cards and collectibles, some clothing, money out of wallet and took the papers which were my old neighbor's opinions of my first book. Those two also went in the South Hill, US bank and I know it had to be the manager Beth who give the brown, Duryea my money.

When I conversed with, Jesus about, I was told the day my account gets closed I'll be shown visible proof on who gave him the money. When it was banked at, Beth's desk was about five steps in and ten to fifteen feet to the right. I went there for about twelve years and not once did I see her behind a teller window but as my evidence that was seen.

Duryea Coleman's a child molesting sick bastard. He met Britany on 4th of July at my then fourteen-year-old sisters' friend, Sarah's party, and is eleven years older than her. For physical proof, their daughter, Miahona' was born in 2004 and Britany arrived in 1986. With being sick at mind he's beaten her harshly many times.

Him, David Lee Schuck and Antonio Phillips all beat my sister, and reason she didn't leave is sin within her. The majority of that was deposited through physical relationships with, Duryea.

About eight years after I got home from, Good Samaritan my stellar hearing ease dropped and before she caught on I heard, her and Duryea talking about what they did.

Their child, Miahona' Coleman is very vindictive. Reason her brother, Preston has awesome manners and is well respectable she can't rely on the excuse that the one who's both their mom and did the same thing to him, bad behavior is because my sisters' absence. People aren't aware or can't see in the spirit like me but a main source for Miahona's behavior is what's within her manipulative boyfriend, Tyreque. When she wasn't with him stuff didn't go missing but even though I bought him a new x box game and controller while dating, her characters wavery between nice and mean. But also, her upbringing is the root: lazy parents.

My religious mom assumes he's innocent but he twists and turns things; which makes it seem satisfying to his girlfriend. Which is also why mom doesn't stretch but sticks to what's black & white. Meaning if it makes sense and on paper, like all religious it must be true.

To verify myself when her and I went to the mall, at two different times I pointed out two cute teenagers and asked if she thinks their more handsome than her boyfriend? When, 'yes I do,' was heard I knew my thoughts were right in line.

On the fourth of the same month an email from, isaveyou@gmail.com gave me the address and the description. Later that month my former dishonest caregiver, Dennis Eicher who asked to grab my penis, drove me to, Bob's Sports Cards, which was on the corner of 5th and Proctor. An employee attempted to deceive me with the words, 'the owner isn't here and I've never heard of those two.'

When my caregiver took me there were no, going out of business postings anywhere. Two months later I went to my previous dentist and passed where the card shop **used to be**.

Because the law only believes the facts if such are black and white; there you go!

The attacks by sin aren't finished. My mom banks at, US bank and because there is liked it was referred. At first and even after I handed in the first check everything was good. But even though checks from, Mary Ann C. Bohavente from, Goose Creek South Carolina, Joseph Edward from, Atlanta, Georgia and Michael Crandell from Santa Barber, California had verifying letters, Beth A. Duat found them as fraud and pocketed the money. And Beth herself verified what I already knew. Five years after I handed in the check from, Mary Ann I was told it was fraud and she pocketed the remaining money in my account, $3,755.

Around two years six months following closing my account I signed up and told, United Nations I'd been cheated and stolen from. The brain injury I endured caused my memory to be weaker than poor. In having the mindset, US bank was banked at I gave the address of one that's about ten miles from the one, Beth works at. Couple months following one year later the, US bank in, Albertson's calls me and notifies me, the check from, United Nations in New York, New

York was mailed there; for me. Reason I'm very familiar with sin, it was picked up, therefore I asked, what's your name? Tamera Grothes, said the woman.

After informing, she has to check and see if it's good we hung up. Note: each check I turned into, Beth took one to two weeks but, Tamera called back in little bit past twenty minutes.

On, July 4th of 2000 I knew my ex, Brandy Hess was desperate and just fishing, in her attempt to deceive with, 'I'm pregnant.' Meaning I wasn't driving crazy but emts, Bill Cunningham and Isaac Knots dropped me on my head, then staged the accident. Reason, Highline hospital's doctors, dr. Wuss, dr. Mary, and dr. Stevens were inattentive my bone structure was really contorted and in areas my brain forgot how to function, being spaced out I went through five seizures and it's decreased but still I deal with sins torment while I'm awake.

The hate for me isn't over yet. In two thousand eighteen I was diagnosed with lung and bladder cancer, but thank goodness for my mother's thorough studies. Therefore, in all ways sugar was subtracted from my diet. Which resulted with, six months afterwards, entirely there wasn't any trace of cancer in my body.

To all victims and ones who know someone with, when you **starve something eventually it dies**, and **sugar's what cancer feeds on**.

CPSIA information can be obtained
at www.ICGtesting.com
Printed in the USA
BVHW022158051022
648812BV00012B/102

9 798885 908115